Johannes Justus Lansperger, Lord Philip Howard Earl of Arundel

An epistle of Jesus Christ to the faithful soul

Johannes Justus Lansperger, Lord Philip Howard Earl of Arundel
An epistle of Jesus Christ to the faithful soul
ISBN/EAN: 9783337729271

Printed in Europe, USA, Canada, Australia, Japan

Cover: Foto ©Lupo / pixelio.de

More available books at **www.hansebooks.com**

AN
EPISTLE OF JESUS CHRIST
TO THE
FAITHFUL SOUL,

That is devoutly affected towards Him:

Wherein are contained certain divine infpirations teaching a man to know himfelf, and inftructing him in the perfection of true Piety.

Written in *Latin* by the devout fervant of Chrift, JOANNES LANSPERGIUS, *a Charter-Houfe Monk;*

and Tranflated into *Englifh* by

LORD PHILIP, XIXTH EARL OF ARUNDEL.

(*Reprinted from the Edition of* 1610.)

Dedicated, by Permiffion, to
HIS GRACE THE DUKE OF NORFOLK,
Earl Marfhal of England, &c., &c.

NEW YORK:

Howard, Earl of Arundel," *by His Grace the late Duke of Norfolk.*(1)

"But after his condemnation he ſpent betwixt four and five hours every morning in prayer and meditation, and betwixt three and four in the afternoon. The reſt of his time, excepting that little he ſpent in walking or ſome other corporal exerciſe appointed by the phyſicians, he beſtowed either in writing or tranſlating books of piety. One book, *Lanſpergius*, containing *An Epiſtle of Jeſus Chriſt to ye Faithful Soul*, he tranſlated out of Latin into *Engliſh*, and cauſed it to be printed, for the furtherance of devotion."—Page 106.

"Philip Howard, nineteenth Earl of Arundel, was ſon of Thomas, Duke of Norfolk, and the Lady Mary Fitz-Alan. This Book, and its author, are unnoticed by Walpole or Park. The latter and Mr. Heber aſſure me they have never heard of or ſeen another copy."—*Note by Dr. Bliſs.*

The above note is inſide the cover of the copy in the Britiſh Muſeum. A copy of this tranſlation, however, is in the poſſeſſion of the Right Hon. Lord Petre. Another copy of the ſame edition as that in the Britiſh Muſeum (1610) is in the Library of the Dominican Priory, Woodcheſter. Another copy (imperfect) of an earlier edition, Antwerp, 1595, is in the poſſeſſion of Alfred Blount, Eſq.—*Publiſher's Note.*

(¹) London : Hurſt and Blackett, 1857.

TO

HIS GRACE, THE MOST NOBLE

HENRY FITZ-ALAN HOWARD, DUKE OF NORFOLK,

EARL MARSHAL, PREMIER DUKE AND EARL OF ENGLAND, &c. &c. &c.

THIS REPRINT OF A TRANSLATION FROM THE LATIN OF JOANNES LANSPERGIUS, MADE BY HIS MOST VIRTUOUS ANCESTOR, THAT NOBLE CONFESSOR OF THE FAITH,

THE LORD PHILIP, XIXTH EARL OF ARUNDEL,

DURING HIS CAPTIVITY IN THE TOWER OF LONDON,

IS, BY KIND PERMISSION,

DEDICATED

BY HIS OBEDIENT AND HUMBLE SERVANT,

JOHN PHILP.

The Epiftle Dedicatory.

(*Third Edition*, 1610.)

TO

THE REVEREND MOTHER

AND DEVOUT POOR SISTERS

Of the Holy ORDER OF S. CLARE, in the firft Englifh Convent erected in Graveling.

THIS brief but moft excellent EPISTLE OF JESUS CHRIST TO THE FAITHFUL SOUL (Religious Poor Sifters), worthy, no doubt, both of the Author's piety and Tranflator's virtue, being fo much by you and others defired, and now the third time printed, I have thought it both to your profit and for your confolation to prefent the fame unto you, as a mirror or looking-glafs, who, being now entered into the path of virtue, do earneftly endeavour to arrive to the height of Christian Religious Perfection; especially at this time, when almost all virtuous life and devotion in our country, by the unfortunate sway of Schism and Heresy, lieth, as it were, languishing, and sick even unto death itself. That by this means some little sparks of piety may be conserved alive within the embers of your religious breasts, thereby to enkindle and inflame the hearts, not only of those who, by this your virtuous example, shall follow your footsteps, but of others also into whose hands this Golden Treatise, so particularly due unto yourselves for the rare documents of perfection it containeth, shall happily come. Our sweet Saviour increase daily your earnest desire of Religious Piety, and preserve you ever, *Amen.*

Your servant in Christ Jesus,

The Epistle of the Author.

TO

THE VENERABLE MOTHER

AND

RELIGIOUS VIRGINS

Of the Order called *Premonstratensis*, dedicated to Christ in the Monastery of *Hensberch*.

JOANNES LANSPERGIUS,

Prior of the Carthusians, *wisheth grace and peace.*

NO man I suppose to be so ignorant (devout Virgins) as to think this ensuing speech or exhortation, ascribed to our Blessed Saviour Christ, was either spoken by His own mouth or made by Him personally when He lived here on earth; but that it is therefore styled with so glorious a title because it containeth that very Doctrine which is truly and really Christ's, as His divine in-

fpirations do daily witnefs. Which Doctrine is not only felt inwardly in our hearts, but is alfo here fet down in characters, as if Chrift Himfelf did feem to fpeak unto us, both in word and writing. And, indeed, man's mind is fo much the more vehemently ftirred up to liften and obey, by how much he doth now feel and receive this Doctrine, as it were, not from man, but from Chrift. For who can doubt but that every doctrine doth fo much the more delight and perfuade the reader, by how much he who teacheth the fame is of greater dignity and eftimation? Seeing, then, we greatly wifh that the hearts of all fuch as fhall read this book fhould be enlightened with the Spirit of Chrift, we do therefore perfuade all men to read the fame, not in our own but in Chrift's name, whereby every one may make himfelf worthy of fuch a Spirit. For the dulnefs of our Spirit, fo long as we remain in this our corruptible body, hath this property, that it is fooneft moved, ftirred up, and extended towards God with fenfible things, and fuch as are more familiar to human underſtanding. And for this caufe hath the Holy Church received the divers ceremonies in her Divine Service which now-a-days ſhe uſeth, as organs, ſinging, and other the ſundry ornaments thereof; as alſo in like manner are the Images and Pictures of Chriſt and of His Saints, before which the common people do exerciſe their devotion; as when, in beholding them, they are either moved with the remembrance of Chriſt's benefits towards them, or ſtirred up to imitate their examples of ſanctity, or elſe, turning themſelves to Chriſt, do offer up the worſhip of their devotion, not to ſtocks or ſtones, but unto Him whoſe perſon the image repreſenteth. For although we are not ignorant that the picture of Chriſt which we ſee is not Chriſt, yet, notwithſtanding, the devotion of him that prayeth before it doth no otherwiſe worſhip it than Chriſt Himſelf, whoſe picture it is; becauſe his mind is not then carried (or fixed) upon the picture, but upon Him whom it repreſenteth. In like manner may this Epiſtle or Exhortation of Jeſus Chriſt be read; not for that it was either written or spoken by Himself, but as it were by Him; seeing that whatsoever is here either taught or said is daily spoken by Christ inwardly to the devout soul, His Spouse.

You, therefore, devoted Virgins of Christ, who have contemned the vanities of this world, read these Exhortations of your Spouse, Christ Jesus, which, by a secret kind of inspiration (if you mark it) He continually breathes into your hearts. And in so doing shall you read those things whereof you may be inwardly admonished, if you will vouchsafe to give ear, and hearken what is said. For that herein is contained a Rule to live rightly and piously in the service of God, instructing you in all spiritual conversation. And for this cause have I thought it convenient to write and dedicate the same to your Holy Congregation, imitating herein the devotion of our Blessed *F. Denis of Ruremond*, no less famous for sanctity of life than learning, who, whilst he lived, dedicated many devout works unto consecrated Virgins, and especially to your Holy Convent; as for example, *Of the Profession of Nuns; Of Lively Mortification, and Internal Reformation; Of Spiritual Profit and Watch over the Heart;* &c. Therefore, when as I perceive that you defire nothing more than to have fome chafte and pious doctrine inftilled into you (for which caufe you do fo greatly honour all thofe that be devoutly learned), I doubt not but that, this your defire being fatisfied, you will transfer your cogitations from men to God. Defire, therefore, earneftly this His doctrine, and think that Chrift fpeaketh unto you in thefe Exhortations, as it were in an Epiftle from Himfelf.—*Farewell.*

A Table of the Chapters

Contained in the enfuing Treatife.

                                                     Page

N Epiftle or Exhortation of Jesus Christ *to the Soul that is Devoutly Affected* 1

Chap. I.
A Rule for a Spiritual Life 22

Chap. II.
How we muft Mortify all Unlawful Defires and Wicked Inclinations 27

Chap. III.
How a Man ought to Govern his Tongue . 30

Chap. IV.
Of the Contemplative Life, which is wholly withdrawn from the Cares and Affairs of this prefent World 33

Chap. V.
How we ought to Judge no Man . . . 36

Chap. VI.
How we ought to Fight againft Vice . . 41

Chap. VII.
How we muft fly the Occafions of Temptation 63

A Table of Chapters.

Page

Chap. VIII.
When Spiritual Temptations are to be Conquered 66

Chap. IX.
How we ought to take heed of Envy . . 72

Chap. X.
How we muſt fly Singularity 73

Chap. XI.
Of the Honour, Reverence, and Worſhip which we ought to exhibit unto the MOTHER OF GOD 74

Chap. XII.
Of Senſible Devotion 79

Chap. XIII.
How we muſt prepare ourſelves when we come to receive the BLESSED SACRAMENT . . 82

Chap. XIV.
Of Diſcretion 88

Chap. XV.
How we ought in all things to conform our ſelves unto CHRIST 94

Chap XVI.
Of Poverty 95

Chap. XVII.
Of Humility 100

Chap. XVIII.
How Humility is to be Obtained . . . 102

A Table of Chapters.

	Page

CHAP. XIX.
How we ought not to care for Men's Judgments 113

CHAP. XX.
Of Obedience 120

CHAP XXI.
How we muſt Mortify our own Will and Deſire 127

CHAP. XXII.
Of the Conſideration of GOD'S Providence . 138

CHAP. XXIII.
How we muſt bear Adverſity 145

CHAP. XXIV.
Of Wanting of Conſolation 157

CHAP. XXV.
Of Inward Peace and Meekneſs of Heart . 160

CHAP. XXVI.
Of the Love which we ſhould bear towards our Neighbour 163

CHAP. XXVII.
Of the Purity of the Heart 167

CHAP. XXVIII.
How we ought to refer all the Good Things we receive to the Goodneſs of GOD . . . 170

CHAP. XXIX.
How Divine Inſpirations ought to be Obſerved, and the Grace of GOD not Neglected . . 180

A Table of Chapters.

CHAP. XXX.
How we must Employ the Gifts of GOD which we receive to the Benefit of Others . . 186

CHAP. XXXI.
Of Poverty in Spirit 192

CHAP. XXXII.
Of the Love of GOD 194

CHAP. XXXIII.
Of the Praise of GOD 208

CHAP. XXXIV.
Of the Exercise of the Love and Praise of GOD 218

CHAP. XXXV.
Of the Transformation of Man . . . 227

The Conclusion 236

Two Rules of Direction for a Man's Life . 240

An Instruction or Rule for such as are Weak and Imperfect, and but New Beginners in GOD'S Service 247

Another Instruction or Rule for such as with a more fervent Zeal and Spirit do earnestly labour to attain to Perfection . . . 254

A very short Exercise of Love to GOD the Father, GOD the Son, and GOD the Holy Ghost, the most Blessed Trinity, and One true GOD 271

AN
Epistle of Jesus Christ
TO THE
Faithful Soul.

JESUS CHRIST, THE SAVIOUR OF THE WORLD
AND KING OF HEAVEN AND EARTH;

Being ready to embrace thofe that earneftly and truly defire His grace, with His merciful and fatherly arms, wifheth to His Spoufe, that is, to the Soul which loveth him (for whofe fake He willingly fuffered death that He might unite her to Himfelf) all perfect and true felicity.

MY dearly beloved Daughter, I have fpoken to thy heart by fecret infpirations, but thou wouldeft never give ear unto my motions; wherefore, fince thou didft care little to answer me, much lefs to obey me, I am enforced by

the great love I bear thee, to write unto thee; that at the least thou mayest be content to read what thou didst neglect to hear, and by reading both better bear away my exhortation, and more deeply imprint it in thy mind. For that charity which moved me to offer myself, not only to all danger, but even to death itself, for thy sake, will not suffer me to leave anything undone that may tend to the furtherance of thy salvation. And although thou dost not in any sort requite my love, because thy heart is inclined to outward, vain, and transitory things, and so by that means too much affected and addicted to my creatures; yet I cannot withdraw that charity, wherewith I am always ready to embrace thee, which exceedeth the love of any father or mother towards their children, or of any earthly parent whatsoever. For I am not only willing to grant thee my grace and favour, but desirous to accept thee for my spouse, and will daily enrich thee with greater and better blessings than any that this world can yield thee, if thou wilt follow my counsel. But for that thou hast contemned me when I came to vifit thee, and haft not hearkened to my infpirations, thou art become by this evil cuftom of thine, fo much diftracted in thy foul, and fo far befide thyfelf, as thou art neither able to conceive what thou haft loft, nor yet the mifery wherein thou art, and the lefs that thou doft bewail and lament thine own mifery, the more doth thy cafe deferve to be pitied and lamented.

2. What fhall I fay, O my daughter? Thou fhouldft be an example to others, and thy life an inftruction to thofe that go aftray. The fweet favour of thy good converfation ought to be a wholefome medicine for the curing of fuch as are weakened with infection of fin, and thy words as a confuming fire, to inflame the hearts ot thofe that hear them. But now thou art thyfelf fo corrupted with the defire of childifh vanities, fo bufied with a multitude of unprofitable matters, and fo fubject to many hurtful paffions, as thou art diftracted in thy foul, and haft fo much polluted it with filthinefs, as it is poffeffed with wandering thoughts and vain imaginations.

Self-love doth as yet reign in thee, and till thou mortify that, thou canſt never enter into my chamber, or be partaker of my delights. So thou, who oughteſt to teach others, ſtandeth now in need of being taught thyſelf. I write this, not to the end that I mean to rejeƈt thee, but becauſe I would let thee know how far thou haſt erred, and am deſirous that thou ſhouldſt underſtand thy own loſs and danger; and I do not only allure thee, but I do alſo urge thee forward to return from thence, home again unto me.

3. Whereſoever thou art, whatſoever thou doſt, or whitherſoever thou goeſt, my eye is never off from thee, looking and ſearching into all thy aƈts, all thy motions, and all the ſecret intentions of thy heart. And if at any time I ſpy in any of theſe the leaſt unfaithfulneſs to me, who am moſt faithful, I am juſtly offended and angry. For I did ſuffer not only with all patience, but even with all willingneſs, many affronts, reproaches, griefs, and torments for thy ſake.

4. O, my moſt dear daughter, to paſs over in ſilence all the pains and torments

To the Faithful Soul.

which I did endure, tell me, I pray thee, what man would have fuffered fo many and fo great difgraces for his friend as I did for thee? And yet I endured them when thou waft mine enemy, when thou hadft done no good at all, when thou didft neither love nor know me, yea before thou wert born did I love thee, and fuffer thefe grievous and innumerable torments for thee? Why then wilt thou turn away thyfelf from me? Why doft thou feek quietnefs without me? Thou art fickly, and yet wilt wander abroad: If I forfake thee, who will receive thee? Who can cure thee? Alas, my daughter, how far art thou deceived! Whither thou turneft thine eyes, or upon whatfoever thou doft fix thy mind, yet thou fhalt find no peace, no joy, nor any reft, but in me only. Thy fenfes deceive thee, and they which feem to love thee do abufe thee, and thou alfo doft deceive thyfelf, when thou refufeft a fovereign medicine that would help thee, and receiveft rank poifon, which will kill thee.

5. Alas, my Daughter, alas my Spouse;

I know how often beautiful and goodly things in ſhew, but vain things indeed, (which when they profeſs moſt love and faith unto thee are moſt ready to beguile thee) do allure thy ſenſes and draw thy affection, and how often alſo they deceive thee with their ſnares, and lead thee from me with their guiles. O, dear Daughter, remember that thou art a Spouſe, and let not the love of any other thing but only thy husband enter into thy heart. Deſire nothing but his favour, that thou mayeſt be beautiful in his eyes, and pleaſe him, and be for ever beloved of him. I ſtand deſiring thee, and waiting for thee; I wiſh that thou wouldſt return unto me with all thy heart, and forſaking all theſe vanities, apply thyſelf wholly to devotion, and give thyſelf daily to humility; that I might then vouchſafe to talk with thee in more familiar ſort, and rejoice thy mind with far better and purer delights than thoſe wherein thou haſt lain drowned.

6. I require no multitude of works at thy hands, wherewith to trouble thee, but a chaſte, faithful, and pure heart, which

may seek to please me, and not delight itself. I desire a sincere love, and a fervent devotion, that is, a ready and forward will to honour and obey me, and a sincere and pure intention in performing of all those things that I command. I wish that thy heart should be clear and free from any other love whatsoever, and if thou wouldst present it to me in this sort, I would endow thee with greater consolations and far more excellent blessings, than either thou darest presume to desire or art able to conceive. I am a husband that is bashful, and therefore will never come unto thee, when I see thee busied with other matters altogether vain and unprofitable. When I come I must find thee alone, for I stand knocking at thy door, being very weak and quaking for cold, even in the same form that I carried, when I was unloosed from the pillar whereto, being bound, I was scourged and wounded for thy sake. And this I do, that I may make an impression of myself in thy mind, wounded as I was, and that thou, embracing me with the arms of thy love, I may unite thee unto me, and inflame thee with my wounds, that do yet burn with the fervent heat of that charity which I bear towards thee.

7. Oh, if thou wouldſt acknowledge me for thy husband, and love me as thou oughteſt to do, wouldſt thou not both quickly draw me into thy heart, and alſo before I came, with a moſt deſirous will, attend and long for my coming; and wouldſt thou not then clothe the naked, and give fire to warm him that is cold, that thou mighteſt be made worthy to receive again the chaſte embracings of my love, and to enjoy the ſweet taſte of my ſpirit?

8. How much it would pleaſe me that thou hadſt a certain and firm truſt in me, and wert as willing to be with me, as I am deſirous to be with thee, ſeeing all my delight conſiſteth in being with the Children of men.[1] So ſhould the fortitude of thy mind be daily augmented, and the true ſweetneſs of thy ſoul continually increaſed. But this truſt in me can never be without a diſtruſt in thyſelf, and both theſe graces are only obtained by poverty

[1] Prov. viii. 31.

of fpirit, which is a most precious jewel. But I know well enough what doth withhold thee from attaining to this virtue; thy heart is overlaid with the love of this world, and by that means infected with fuch an extreme coldnefs, as it maketh thee to loathe and abhor the Word of God, which is the food of thy foul. But if thou defire to increafe in virtue, and to ftrengthen thy mind with the following of that courfe, thou muft receive the Word of God greedily, digeft it perfectly, and ftill retain the nourifhment of that within thee.

9. The reafon, therefore, that thou canft not thirft after my juftice is, becaufe thou art already filled with the cold meats of worldly converfation and vanity, and that is the caufe alfo why thefe things do delight thee, which favour neither of piety nor devotion. Simplicity of heart is loathfome unto thee, and the exercife of holy meditations, thou accounteft as time loft. Thy mind being laden with the cares of this world, cannot afcend up unto me. For although thou raifeft it by force for a

while, yet it prefently falleth down again into her earthly cogitations; fo as thy foul being diftracted, thy heart inconftant, thy mind wavering, and thy defires enfnared with the love of worldly pleafure: thou art troubled when thou art awake, and not quiet when thou art afleep.

10. And when thou lieft in this mifery, O unwife Daughter, then thou complaineft that thou art dry and barren, without my confolations. If this did happen unto thee, by the means of my Providence, (as it hath to many other of my friends) and not by thine own negligence, there were no reafon why the wanting of this fenfible grace of mine fhould moleft thy foul. But feeing thy own floth and negligence is the caufe that thou lieft languifhing in this barren drynefs,—if thou defire my confolation,—if thou wifheft for my coming,—if thou doft long to be united unto me, thou muft forfake all thofe vanities, that do pleafe thee without me, and only ftudy to ferve me, endeavouring continually to perform thofe things which agree beft with my liking, and are moft pleafing unto

me. And making this thy chiefeſt care, thou muſt labour with all thy force and might to fee my will, as near as thou canſt, in all creatures fulfilled. Moreover, in doing hereof, let thy whole ſtudy be to content me, and to rely only upon me. So ſhalt thou find my preſence more often with thee, and by it thy ſpirit ſhall be, as it were, made drunk with joy; thy conſcience ſhall be comforted; thy heart quieted; and thou ſhalt then poſſeſs the perfect reſt of moſt ſweet contemplation.

11. Oh, if thou hadſt once come into that wine-cellar, out of doubt thou wouldſt even with a certain thirſtineſs, more earneſtly defire to be there and more often. But no man can enter into it, ſaving ſuch as defire me above all things, love me above all things, eſteem me above all things, and make account of me as all in all. For he that findeth no other confolation but in me, he that thinketh himſelf unworthy to receive any confolation from me, nay, he that defireth affliction ſo much in this world that he taketh himſelf to be wronged, when I ſend him any confolation

at all, and doth as willingly accept it at my hands, when I leave his foul barren without any comfort, as when I replenish it with my confolation, to whom all joy without me is a torment, having his mind wholly fixed upon me, and his defire only bent to ferve me. Such men as thefe are, I fay, my fpecial friends, at whofe door I do freely knock, and willingly enter; thefe are the men to whom I gladly offer myfelf, and impart my fecrets. Thefe men I am wont to vifit in fundry ways, as feemeth fitteft in my judgment, by ftirring them up in fuch manner as is meet and agreeable for the devotion and love which they bear me.

12. Sometimes I prefent myfelf to the eyes of their fouls, wounded, naked, and tormented in all my members, and that they may find greater comfort in the love they bear me, I fhew them my wounds, to the end that they may touch them, bathe them, cleanfe them, kifs them, and embrace them. And although their devotion in this behalf may feem to worldly men ridiculous, becaufe they know not what it meaneth,

yet it is moſt acceptable to me, and moſt profitable to them. For then I begin to forget all the pains which I have ſuffered, and alſo all the faults which ſuch a ſpouſe of mine hath committed againſt me, and do wholly bend myſelf to comfort her with my ſpirit and to lighten her with my grace.

13. And although I ſtand not in need of anything, yet I make account I have gained much, when I find ſo great fidelity in my ſpouſe, as ſhe loveth me better than either herſelf, or all the world besides. But unthankfulneſs doth offend me, as much as fidelity doth content me, and is of all things moſt grievous unto me, becauſe by it they ſeek to renew (as much as lieth in them) the griefs of my Paſſion, and vexations of my mind; ſeeing, I perceive, that all is loſt, which I did with an unſpeakable charity endure for them. Therefore, whether outward affliction of thy body, or inward affliction of thy mind, happen unto thee, ſeek not for external comforts, which are nothing worth, but in all thy diſtreſs fly unto me, and make no complaint of thy grief unto any man, but to me only.

For what greater help can men yield thee than in giving thee fair words? If thou haſt a Ghoſtly Father or Confeſſor, I forbid thee not to difcloſe it unto him, but I exhort thee to lay open before him the ſecrets of thy heart, and to direct thyſelf in all reſpects according to his counſel, without yielding any way to fatisfy the fury of thy paſſion, or labouring for fome external comfort, or boaſting before others of thoſe vexations which thou doſt ſuffer.

14. Declare to me in ſecret that which thou wouldſt complain of before men, committing thyſelf and all things to my Providence, being quiet without any care or perturbation of thy mind. Thou ſhalt find, believe me, a happy peace in thy ſoul, and great conſolation by this courſe at my hands, although not ſuch, peradventure, at all times as thou doſt imagine or wiſh for, yet ſuch as may moſt of all conform thee to my will and pleaſure.

15, Oh! if thou wert taught and accuſtomed by thine own experience in all worldly things which trouble thee to have thine eye only fixed upon me, to fly unto me for refuge, to hope in my mercy with a patient expecting of the fame, to rely upon me, and withal, to conceive with how fatherly and loving a mind I fend thee adverfity for thy benefit; there fhould be no tribulation fo great that thou wouldft not with all gladnefs and willingnefs accept; yea, and prefer it before all joy or confolation whatfoever. For albeit thou fhouldft receive no other commodity by it, yet this were fufficient to comfort and rejoice thy mind that it is a fulfilling of my will. If my will be done, it doth always pleafe the faithful foul, more than the receiving of any other benefit, although in truth my will be never but to do that which may be moft for her intereft.

16. It will alfo help thee very much for retaining a quiet mind in all adverfity, to lay before thy eyes the acts and miferies of my life, and evermore to carry within thee a lively reprefentation thereof. For if thou do imprint this in thy mind, it will make thee think all bitter things fweet. Meditate, therefore, at all times upon my torments, and defire at my hands continu-

ally, with sighs and tears, that I may vouchsafe to make a strong and an effectual impression in thy heart of my wounds and passion, that thou mayest see me crucified at all times, and in all places, with a heart that doth even suffer with me; and let the lively representation hereof banish from thy soul all other imaginations whatsoever. If thou return in this sort from all outward to inward things, and shalt dwell within thine own self; if thou behold in thy heart my grievous torments, and myself crucified; if thou hear me cry, when I was replenished with all sorrow and bitterness, and not relieved with any consolation from my father: *My God, my God, why hast thou forsaken me:* thou shalt (being inflamed with the virtue of my passion) have a desire to imitate me, to suffer for me, and to serve me without any comfort at all, in contempt and resignation of thyself.

17. They that serve me with this mind, and are united unto me for mere love only, and continue faithful unto me without any other respect but to please me, and to have my will wholly fulfilled in them, these

To the Faithful Soul.

thou hadſt forgotten all other things whatſoever, and wert out of this world ; in quietneſs and ſilence ſpeak to me only, and hearken unto me wholly.

6. Never ſtrive with any man in words, neither ſeek ſtiffly to maintain thy own mind or opinion ; ſuffer every man to have his ſaying, if thou canſt not diſſuade him by gentle words or do him good by ſome mild exhortation. And, to conclude, reſolve thyſelf neither to diſpute in words, neither yet reaſon in thine own thoughts againſt him, but refer all things unto me, and live thou in all ſilence of thy tongue, and in all quietneſs of thy heart.

Chap. IV.

Of the Contemplative Life which is wholly withdrawn from the Cares and Affairs of this Preſent World.

FLY the ſociety and familiarity of men, and when thou art not otherwiſe enforced by neceſſity for my honour, or for thy neighbour's ſalvation, be always alone, for when thou art alone then will I reveal myfelf unto thee. Solitarinefs, filence, purity, and fimplicity of heart, do prepare a place for me to dwell in. Keep thyfelf, therefore, withdrawn from all creatures, in filence and quietnefs of heart. Neither vouchfafing to confent, nor yet to hearken to the unlawful appetites of thy will, the wandering cogitations of thy mind, or the vain defires of thy heart. For thy nature (I know) is ever inclined to delight in confolation, and is always occupied, fometimes with outward labour in thy body, and fometimes with inward care in thy mind, feeking confolation in my creatures, whereby thou comeft to be many and fundry ways diftracted.

2. Remember thou, therefore, to ftrive with all thy force againft all thy fenfual and carnal inclinations, and keep thyfelf alone, being withdrawn from all creatures, and remaining ever, both in outward folitarinefs of thy body and inward contemplation of thy mind, as far as difcretion, which muft be thy guide, obedience to thy fuperiors, and charity to thy neighbours, will permit thee. Take care, alfo, as much as

conveniently thou mayeſt, not to give others, by thy example, any occaſion of often meeting, or common familiarity, becauſe it doth very much hinder the ſpiritual courſe of life, which is never ſo free from any impediment, nor ſo apt to profit itſelf, as when it is ſeparated from all ſorts of men, and all kind of buſineſs. Yet, howſoever thou ſhalt chance to be, either living amongſt men, or ſequeſtered from the ſociety of men, remain with me always alone, recollected within thy own ſoul, and withdrawn not only from all other creatures, but even from thine own ſelf; that is, from all liking to procure thine own pleaſure, from all care to ſeek thine own commodity, and from all deſire to ſerve thy own appetite.

3. Perſuade thyſelf that thou art left alone in this world, and haſt nothing to care for but me, and, therefore, think of no other matter, and deal with no other creature but with me only. Examine not other men's actions, and trouble not thyſelf with other men's affairs. If thou ſeeſt that which is good, embrace it, and let it edify

thee; if thou feeft that which is evil, leave it, but give no judgment of it.

4. Beware of obferving, marking, examining, or judging of fuch men's fpeeches, actions, and manners, as cannot by their holy and good example edify thee. Nay, be fo far from doing this, as defire never to hear or underftand them, but rather feek by all means not to know them at all. And if thou fhalt happen by any chance to hear them, root them out of thy heart, and endeavour to forget them as foon as thou canft, efpecially if thou ftandeft in danger, by that means, to offend in the breach of charity, or to conceive a worfe opinion of thofe parties.

Chap. V.

How we ought to Judge no Man.

THINK ill of no man, and although he feemeth to thee to be wicked, yet believe that he hath been fuffered to fall by fome fecret and hidden providence of mine, for the attaining of greater humility in himſelf, and procuring of greater profit to his ſoul. And thou oughteſt neither to judge nor yet deſpiſe him, but lament rather thy own ingratitude towards me, becauſe my grace only doth uphold thee, as it were, violently againſt thy will; and think that without it thou ſhouldſt fall into greater and more heinous ſins than any other. Therefore, ſay unto thyſelf: If this man had received ſo much grace as I have done, he would have ſerved God a great deal more devoutly, and been more thankful unto him, than I have been.

2. Believe alſo, that as ſoon as I look upon him with the eyes of my mercy, he will preſently repent and amend; or elſe, that he is already reformed and made more holy than thoſe that deſpiſe him. Wherefore, aſcribe thy ill-conceit of him to thine own fault and raſh judgment, and reprehend thyſelf ſharply becauſe thou haſt thought amiſs of thy neighbour, and done him wrong. Rancour, hatred, bitterneſs, and envy, do many times hide themſelves under the colour of zeal, which do make men think, not only every defeƈt and light fault of their

neighbour to be grievous, but also to judge their virtues to be vices, their sights being dimmed with the foggy mist of malice and envy.

3. Take special heed, therefore, that thou neither reprehend nor accuse any man, nor yet either speak or hear of any man's faults when thou art angry. Beware also that thou dost not at that time seek to gall him, gainsay him, or grieve him with any word or show of thine; neither yet by chiding to procure humility and shame in him; or to declare that thou hast taken him in a fault worthy of reprehension, and meet to be spoken of. And chiefly abstain from doing of this, as long as displeasure, bitterness, or any troubled and unquiet passion doth remain in thy heart against him, and as long as thou dost desire to make others note him for his faults and offences, because thou hast neither zeal of charity, nor a sincere intention in thee at that time. For if thou hadst, thou wouldst rather be sorrowful, and lament with him for his sins, and seek as much as thou couldst to excuse and cover before others thy brother's or sister's

offence. And if they had made a great fault thou wouldſt then rebuke them in ſecret, not without grief in thy own ſoul, and wouldſt pray earneſtly unto me for them, with a heart that did even ſuffer with them for their offences, and were moſt lovingly and humbly affeƈted towards them.

4. O, my daughter, be diligent to know what thou wanteſt, and what is fit for my ſpouſe. And as for other men's faults, be deaf to hear them, dumb to utter them, and blind to ſee them. Tell me (my daughter) how great regard would a baſhful virgin have of her behaviour, if ſhe ſtood in a king's preſence, and ſaw his eyes continually fixed upon her? After the ſame ſort, think how that I am in all places preſent with thee, and that thou ſtandeſt always in my ſight. Conſider how great modeſty there ought ever to be in thee, how great innocency of life, and, to be ſhort, how great reverence thou oughteſt to carry towards me, who do always behold, and look with my piercing eyes into the depth of all thy aƈts, thoughts, paſſions, words, motions,

intentions, and even the very secrets of thy heart!

5. Presume not, therefore, to do anything in my sight which thou darest not offer to do in the sight of one of my servants that were a very devout man, and so generally accounted, and of all men greatly esteemed; for thou oughtest ever to fear the dreadful presence of my almighty power and infinite Majesty, and to have it at all times, both laid before thy eyes and imprinted in thy heart, that by it thou mayest be stirred up to love and reverence me; and be careful in all things to please me, since thou art continually in my sight.

6. Thou shouldst not have the peace of thy soul, which thou dost in all places desire, to depend upon men's mouths; that is, to be quiet when no man doth gainsay thee, but to rest upon me and a good conscience. Moreover, thou oughtest to mortify that appetite in thyself which doth provoke thee, with an earnest desire and delight, to be beloved and commended of men. Suffer men to be men still, and apply thyself only to love me, that thou mayest be worthy to

stand highly in my favour. Live uprightly with thy neighbour and love him for my sake, neither care thou whether he love thee again or not, but leave it to me, and fly the familiarity both of men and women, but especially of those that be not of thine own sex.

7. If thou hadst as great a care, or, at the least, no less respect to please me than thou hast not to displease men, thou shouldst obtain by it greater consolation in thy soul than if all the world did seek for thy favour.

Chap. VI.

How we ought to Fight against Vice.

BE stout and circumspect, to vanquish and purge thy soul of any imperfection, although it be never so little, for the least sin that offendeth me ought not to seem small in thy eyes, if thou dost perfectly love me. Call to mind the love that thou didst carry towards me heretofore, which made thee to contemn and forsake, for the love of me, thy parents, thy brethren, thy sisters, thy riches, thy honour, and whatsoever else that seemeth delightful in this present world; and to conclude even thyself, that is, thy flourishing youth, and pleasantest years; how cometh it, then, now to pass that thou art vanquished with a most light temptation, and a vile notion of concupiscence?

2. Thou knowest best thyself how weak and negligent thou art for the most part, and how hardly thou art drawn to overcome vice, to beware of those snares which may endanger thy soul, to fly the occasions and provocations of sin, to renounce thy own will, and to amend the imperfections of thy heart. Renew, therefore, thy constant and former determination, resolving to persecute all vice in thyself, and not to suffer anything to remain within thee that is contrary to my will, for any worldly gain whatsoever. Neglect not to do all those things which please me, and follow that course of life which I require at thy hands, and is fit for thy vocation, with all care and diligence. Be careful not to

delay, neither leave thofe things undone which is thy duty to perform, and my right to receive, but do them with courage, ftoutly, willingly, carefully, faithfully, and devoutly.

3. Whenfoever thou findeft in thyfelf the motions of anger, concupifcence, wantonnefs, pride, and fuch like motions of vices, beware that thou doft not fuffer them violently to break out of thee by any word or fhew; but feek, by bridling and refifting them, to fupprefs and extinguifh them. The beft and moft prefent remedy againft all kinds of vice, is to caft thyfelf when thou art tempted proftrate at my feet, with all humility, to confider how thou wert made of nothing, and art nothing but by my grace; to turn unto me wholly, to repofe all thy confidence in me, to call upon me by continual prayer, and perfectly to know that thou canft receive no fuccour nor remedy in this thy diftrefs but from me only.

4. Seek to ftrengthen thine own infirmity in this fort every hour, and renew thy good purpofe, ever perfuading thyfelf that the prefent inftant wherein thou liveft, is the

first time of thy beginning to do well. When it shall seem loathsome to thy nature, or go against thy sensual appetite, to take these labours, to enter into these combats and conflicts, and to do many other things which may seem contrary and grievous to thy mind in this exercise of virtue, ever the more that thine own slothful humour shall repine at them, the more earnestly endeavour thou to overcome and mortify these passions.

5. Be not wearied with so holy a labour, neither cease thou to proceed in so good a course, lest it move me also to stay from pouring the influence of my grace into thee. Be afraid lest that, if thou yield thyself vanquished, or seemest tired by reason of thy sloth, my grace shall forsake thee, and that I will leave thee to follow thy own inventions, and with a dangerous kind of security to satisfy thy own desires, ; for it is a manifest argument that I have then, for thy own deserts, both justly and clearly rejected thee, when thou feelest no worm of conscience gnawing within thee, no remorse for thy sins, nor any fear of my dreadful judgment.

6. Such as are in this ſtate are in a moſt perilous caſe, for when they think peace neareſt unto them, then cometh deſtruction moſt ſudden upon them. Wherefore, fight thou manfully, and violently repreſs thine affections. Wiſh in this ſmall conflict or affliction, how little ſoever it be, to yield me ſome recompenſe, as far as lieth in thy power, for thoſe pains and torments which, both living and dying, I endured for thy ſake.

7. Be never wearied, therefore, with fighting againſt many temptations, give not place, wax not faint, neither ſuffer thou thyſelf to be overcome with weakneſs in thy heart, nor deſperation in thy mind, but perſecute all vice with a continual and mortal hatred, and as often as thou beginneſt to faint, or to decline from thy former determination, ſo often riſe again and make a new reſolution.

8. One thing I muſt needs warn thee of, which hurteth thyſelf and offendeth me, which is, that thou art become ſometimes ſo faint-hearted with thy faults and over-ſights, as that they move thee to waver

in following of the good courſe that thou haſt begun, and almoſt induce thee to deſpair. This is the cauſe that doth make thee ſit ſolitary, pining, and confuming for very grief, and not to return unto me that thou mayeſt riſe again, but even with a kind of deſpair to imagine that all thou haſt done before is utterly loſt and forgotten. And thou ſheweſt thyſelf by this kind of dealing to be proud, becauſe when thou didſt ſeem to ſtand, thou didſt truſt too much in thy own force and ability, and that maketh thee now to be ſo greatly troubled and perplexed in thy mind, becauſe thy hope did fail thee, and it fell out otherwiſe than thou didſt expect or look for.

9. My will is, that thou ſhouldſt not uſe the help of thy own force and endeavour, but utterly to diſtruſt both in them and thyſelf, and to truſt in me only, for, as long as thou thinkeſt otherwiſe, thou art like every hour to come to ruin, until thou learneſt this leſſon, that when thou relieſt upon thyſelf, thine own ſtrength is no greater help unto thee to make thee ſtand upright than if thou wert under-propped

with a broken reed. But defpair not in me, repofing a moft firm hope, and affured confidence in my mercy.

10. And touching thyfelf, I would have thee to defpair after this fort: not to refufe thy own counfel, thy own induftry, thy own travail, and other things of fuch like kind which proceed from thyfelf, but I would have thee continually to ufe them, and yet not to rely upon them, confidently to truft or delight in them, neither yet would I have thee attribute any good thou receiveft to thyfelf, or to thine own diligence; for both thyfelf, and all thefe abilities which thou haft, have not power to make thee withftand the fmalleft fin, except thou be affifted with my grace and mercy. Neither think thou that I will prefently pour into thee, for one earneft prayer, a few tears, or one only conflict againft the temptation of fin, all graces, all virtues, and all good gifts; or that I will for this, fend thee any fudden or extraordinary profit in thy fpiritual courfe of life, or that thou fhalt immediately come to attain to all piety and holinefs.

11. I require at thy hands daily pains, unfeigned humbling of thyself, and a continual fidelity towards me, in fighting against vice. I look for also a firm hope, and an assured trust in my mercy, and a constancy in thee, that will neither be overcome with any assault, nor yet wearied with any travail. And when thou shalt find in thyself all these things which I have named, let there not want a most profound humility, whereby thou mayest be brought perfectly to know thyself, and to confess that, as thou wert made of nothing by my mercy, so thou art nothing but by my grace, attributing nothing to thy own labour and travail, and acknowledging that thou hast deserved nothing, but ascribing thy thirst after justice, and all other good things which thou doest, to me only.

12. Except thou knowest these things thou canst not but err, and must of necessity fall often, until thou come to learn what thou art of thyself, and what thou art by my grace. I forbid thee not, but exhort thee to labour as much as thou canst, and to strive for virtue as much as thou art able;

men, I fay, are my moſt faithful and moſt ſpecial friends. And in what dryneſs or defolation foever they may feem to be, and with what temptations foever they may feem to be overwhelmed, and, as it were, caſt off and forſaken by me, yet in truth they are ſtill mine, becauſe they fight manfully, at their own charge, for my cauſe againſt the whole army of wicked temptations, which do continually aſſault men in the warfare of this prefent world; and will not revolt from my camp, although I fometimes ſtrike and puniſh them.

18. But I do not altogether leave them; for feeing they have conquered all their paſſions, and renounced all their own appetites to pleafe me, and for my fake; yea, and have even altogether forſaken themſelves, and given themſelves only to me, in being fubject only to my will; I cannot hold, but I muſt alſo pour myſelf into them, and both fill, nouriſh, and poſſeſs their fouls with my comfort, which is a hundred times better, purer, and ſweeter, than the worldly pleaſure which they have forſaken. They cannot receive this (as I

have often told thee, and will not ceafe to beat into thy mind) who do feek or accept of any foreign comfort that proceedeth not from me, or is not in me. For my confolation is wonderfully fweet, and beftowed only upon fuch as will admit me, and no other. It is alfo moft pure, and therefore cannot be mixed with any confolation that is derived from my creatures. But why do I fo often repeat thefe things unto thee? Truly I do it to make thee more wife, watchful, and circumfpect, and to the end that thou fhouldft not be fnared with thefe corrupt and earthly delights, nor yet be brought by them to forget me, feeing I can never forget thee, although thy falvation only dependeth upon my Providence, and not mine upon thee in any fort.

19. I wifh alfo that thou fhouldft be continually with me, and by being with me enjoy all perfect felicity. But why do not I fulfil this? Marry, even for thy good, that thou mayeft increafe in virtue and merits, to the great profit of thy foul, and thy greater glory. For thou mayeft by my grace daily increafe in goodnefs and be

made every moment more rich in merit. Wherefore feeing this is fo, how foolifh doft thou think them to be, and how much to be lamented, who do fpend the moft precious time of grace that I have allotted unto them, not only not to my honour and their own profit, but to the heavier aggravating of their damnation by a wicked life? Oh, that thou kneweft how much thou mighteft increafe in the virtues of thy foul, and in merit, by my grace every hour, and alfo how dear a jewel time is, and how damnable the lofs thereof. For thou wouldft then out of doubt take care with more diligence that the fmalleft moment fhould not pafs thee vainly, nor yet flip away without reaping fome benefit to thy foul. With the fun rifing every day, there fhould then arife a new joy in thy mind, that I had granted thee the commodity of that day, and by it fo much longer fpace to honour and ferve me. Think, therefore, and fay every hour unto thyfelf: Our Lord which loveth me hath vouchfafed to give me this hour, this moment, and hath prolonged the courfe of my life hitherto, that I fhould even now begin to turn unto him, and endeavour myself to please him.

20. O my daughter, ever above all things carry this opinion, that the present moment wherein thou livest, is the first time wherein thou beginnest to do well, and contemn all that thou hast done before as nothing worth. What occasion soever, what business soever, what idle time soever, or what other things soever, either may or shall happen unto thee, use them in such sort as thou employ them to my glory, and convert them to some benefit of thy own soul. But this, in this behalf, is sufficient. For I have hitherto stirred thee up, and excited thee to depart from all vanities, with shutting the gates of thy senses against them, and to return unto me with a recollected and quiet mind.

21. It remaineth now that I add unto this, as it were, a rule to teach thee how to live godly, which I have heard thee, by the inspiration of my grace, desire often at my hands. For there remaineth as yet bashfulness in thee (which I like well) and which maketh thee ashamed in the opening of thy

infirmities, faults, errors, and negligences; and also grieved that thou haſt this long time heretofore, and doſt even at this preſent, ſo unworthily uſurp the name of my ſpouſe. But ſeeing thou deſireſt to return into my grace, there is nothing that I likewiſe do more affect or deſire. For what other joy have I in being among you, than to receive every ſinner into my favour? How much more then do I deſire, or rather long (as may in reaſon be juſtly thought), to bring my ſpouſe home unto me, when ſhe goeth aſtray, amongſt the briers and thorns of worldly vanities; nay, I am ſo deſirous to recall thee, as I will preſcribe thee a plain path, wherein (if thou walkeſt) thou ſhalt be ſure to follow my ſteps, and never wander again out of thy way. Come, therefore, unto me, and by thy return procure me a new joy, ſuch as I delight in moſt, and deſire ever to poſſeſs.

Chap. I.

A Rule for Spiritual Life.

MARK well, my daughter, for since I see thee give better care, and apply thy mind with more diligence to carry away my speeches, I will proceed in declaring those things unto thee, which I require at thy hands. Continue, therefore, attentive, and return now wholly unto me, being ready in all things to obey me. Put on a new mind, and hear what I expect that thou shouldst do, and what thou art not able of thyself to do, let prayer assist thee to fulfil.

2. Seek to obtain by prayer whatsoever is necessary for thee, saying: Deliver me from my enemies, O Lord; I fly unto thee for succour; teach me to do thy will, because thou art my God. Leave me not, O Lord my God, and depart not from me; neither yet despise me, who art the God of my salvation. Incline thyself to help me, O Lord, the God of my safety. Behold I

desire to return unto thee, draw me after thee, and never suffer me again to be separated or withdrawn from thee. O my daughter, hearken now to that which I gave in commandment to one of my servants long ago, and endeavour thou also to fulfil it. I said unto him:

> *Use ever silence in thy tongue,*
> *And have compunction in thy mind;*
> *Be humble, courteous, meek, and mild,*
> *If thou in me wilt comfort find.*

3. The same words in the same form do I speak unto thee, having made it in the true measure of a verse, although thou shalt have less need of a measure to direct thee when thou art come to this perfection. But I do not now deliver it unto thee, as framed in measure to please thy ears, but as a sovereign medicine to cure thy soul. I have comprehended all those things, which are necessary for thee, briefly in this verse, that thou mayest more easily retain them in thy memory, and more often meditate upon them in thy mind. For my will is, that thou shouldst altogether apply thy endea-

vour to have a holy compunction for thy sins, and that leaving all other business aside, thou shouldst only attend to a continual and internal conversation, and remaining weaned from all other pleasures, to be recollected into thine own self, and so to continue always free from any distraction or perturbation whatsoever. Be silent in thy tongue, and pure from all filthiness in thy heart. Be humble and meek, and remember to show thyself both courteous and gentle in all thy behaviour towards all sorts of men.

4. First of all, diligently examine thyself, and look most nearly and narrowly into thyself, that thou mayest know what is in thee, which is an impediment to thee, for the receiving of my grace, that is to say, what is in thee which doth displease me, that thou mayest correct and amend it. Consider to what things, and by what means, thou art tempted, and where thou seest thyself most sharply and oftenest tempted, there seek to resist them with greatest diligence, and most earnest endeavour. Where thou findest thyself weaker,

there apply more forcible remedies quickly to vanquiſh them. Where thou perceiveſt any occaſion which moveth thee to ſin, or not to profit in this ſpiritual courſe, there cut off that ſcandal and impediment from thee.

5. Have ſpecial care to preſent unto me a pure heart; free from all uncleanneſs, and neither infected with any inordinate love to my creatures, nor occupied with any unneceſſary buſineſs in this world, and labour evermore with all that thou art able wholly to cleave unto me, and ſtill to rely upon me. The cauſe why I do exhort thee to a continual exerciſe of compunction is that by it thou mayeſt keep thyſelf free from foreign or wandering thoughts, which thou canſt never attain unto, except thou be recollected in thy mind. Neither canſt thou come to be thus recollected, except thou lead an internal and ſolitary life, private to thyſelf and withdrawn from all worldly affairs. Wherefore mark with a watchful eye thoſe vices, concupiſcences, and wicked inclinations which reign in thee, that thou mayeſt never ceaſe with all

thy might to persecute them, and willingly to mortify in thyself all inordinate affections.

6. Many complain that they are unapt for contemplation and spiritual life, but their own negligence and sloth is the cause; for that they will strain themselves no with to conquer their old man, that they may mortify all lusts and concupiscences, but do nourish, cherish, and favour them which they ought to persecute and root out of their minds. Therefore they carry always about with them a heavy burden of unquiet thoughts, filled with labour and vexation; but if thou desire to enjoy me have no peace at all with any vice. Banish from thee all unprofitable discourses, cares, and businesses which yield no benefit at all to thy soul. And never apply thy mind to the thinking of any other matter, nor trouble thyself with any other affairs, but such as tend to my honour, the salvation of thy own soul, or the commodity of thy neighbour, that thou being thus alone, and in this sort retired within thyself, mayest be possessed with me, who will never be matched with any other companion.

Chap. II.

How we muſt Mortify all Unlawful Deſires and Wicked Inclinations.

VOUCHSAFE not to hear, much leſs to read, any news, tidings, or pleaſant hiſtories, which ſerve not to procure a compunction in thy heart, but to delight a curious mind, and afterwards to leave thy ſoul corrupted and infected with ſundry imaginations and vain deſires. Fly any ſpecial familiarity, liking, or converſation with worldly men, that is to ſay, with thoſe that love theſe earthly pleaſures; yea, enter not into any league of familiarity, good- and ſpecial converſation with any ſuch men, whoſe words and deeds do not edify thee in this virtuous courſe, but avoid his company; and mortify all ſenſual love in thyſelf towards any of my creatures.

2. Have ſuch a command over thy belly, as that thou allow it only neceſſary things,

and that alfo not for the pleafing of thy tafte, but for the fuftaining of nature, and for my fake, that by this means thou mayeft not decay, but increafe in ability to ferve me. Moreover, never receive anything to delight thy tafte which is not neceffary and profitable for thy body, and efpecially when thou mayeft obferve this without the breach of brotherly charity. Root out alfo from thy mind after this fort, and fail not both to fly and abhor all pleafant things, all voluptuous things, and all fuch things as feem fweet to thy carnal appetite, as far as difcretion will permit thee, which doth qualify all extremity, ever having a refpect to charity, to infirmity, to the neceffity of nature, and to every other thing that is convenient; and evermore take a fpecial care that in this government of thyfelf thou doft perfecute concupifcence, but not deftroy nature.

3. And as touching thofe things which are neceffary, and yet cannot be received without fome delight, it is fufficient for thee if thou doft not feek that delight but in refpect of me, that is to obey me, who

have committed the care of thy body to thyſelf to refreſh the infirmity of thy nature, ſo as thou takeſt this delight not as a thing which thou wiſheſt for, but as a thing that cannot be ſeparated from that which is neceſſary for man's uſe, admitting it only for neceſſity, and not deſiring it for pleaſure. Therefore, to be ſhort, have ſuch a care and watch over all thy ſenſes, as they may not move or turn themſelves to any vain or unprofitable things. See nothing, touch nothing, know nothing, but that which may be profitable for thy ſoul and my glory.

4. Whereinſoever a man doth follow his own appetite, ſeeking to ſatisfy it of a proper and ſelfwill, that is to ſay, becauſe he will have it ſo, or becauſe he hath a deſire thereunto, he muſt needs offend, for he that deſireth anything in this ſort, whether it be in meat, drink, or any other thing to refreſh nature, or elſe in ſeeking the delight of ſome ſpiritual conſolation, it cannot be done without ſin, becauſe there is in it a particular care to pleaſe his own fancy, which doth divide and ſeparate

him clean from me. Suffer nothing, therefore, to grow in thee, or to be nourifhed by thee, which carrieth any refpect to fatisfy thy own liking or to content thy own will, although it may feem to have an appearance of goodnefs. But thou muft die to all love of thyfelf, and all defire of following thy own appetite, that a naked, a fimple, and a pure charity, without mixture of any other thing whatfoever, and a chafte intention to pleafe me, may ftir, move, and procure thee to all the thoughts thou thinkeft, to all the words thou fpeakeft, and to all the works thou doeft.

Chap. III.

How a Man ought to Govern his Tongue.

HAVE as watchful a care as thou canft over thy tongue, and reftrain it from all liberty, fuffer it to utter nothing but that which is neceffary and well thought of before, and in as few words as it is poffible for thee to

To the Faithful Soul.

comprehend the fame, with all modefty and meeknefs, and without any great noife or loud fpeaking, flying and cutting off, by all the means thou art able, anything that may either occafion or procure thee to fpeak.

2. Abftain from all words that are any way hurtful, backbiting, grudging, unclean, or contentious, as from a mortal fin. Having a fpecial regard to keep thyfelf from all jefting, lightnefs, immoderate laughter, and idle words, and be fo careful in this behalf, as neither thou ufeft them thyfelf, nor yet hear them of any other, as far as it lieth in thy power to avoid it.

3. And to the end thou mayeft be free from that great vice of backbiting, refolve thou in thine own heart never to fpeak anything of thofe who are abfent, but fuch things as thou art fure do tend to the edifying of men's fouls. Ever have fome means ready at hand to break off that talk (if there be any fpeech offered of thofe that be abfent) by bringing aptly in a difcourfe of fome other matter, before there be any word uttered either in the backbiting or difpraifing of them.

4. Take a most diligent and heedful care that thou speakest not thyself, nor sufferest any other to speak, of those who have offended thee, or towards whom thou findest in thy heart no perfect charity, because men may easily fall by that means into the vice of backbiting, while they speak to please thy humour by flattering of thee, and reproaching of those that thou dost mislike. Therefore, never hearken to any accusation that is made of them which are thine enemies, or such as thou dost not love.

5. Endeavour as much as thou canst to remain always in silence (I mean not only the silence of thy tongue, but especially the silence of thy heart), so as there may not be heard within thy soul any sound of unlawful concupiscence, any noise of unquiet passions, or any troublesome stir of wicked affections and inordinate inclinations. Neither suffer thou unprofitable discourses to arise in thine own heart, with any vain fancies, fond imaginations, or the deceitful forms of such things as thou shalt have there represented unto thee; but even as if

and when thou haft done all, truft not in any remedy, nor in any induftry of thy own, that is without me, but hope of this, pray for this, and believe this certainly, that I will never fail to affift thee in all thy diligent and virtuous labours, not in refpect of thine own deferts, but in refpect of the love and charity which I bear thee. For feeing that I have given thee a will, a defire, and an inclination to fight, I will alfo grant thee for thy labour in fight (if thou perfevereft to the end) a crown of glory, a triumph of victory, and a moft happy end of thy combat.

13. Wherefore, whether thou art in war or at peace with thyfelf, whatfoever thou doft determine, whatfoever thou beginneft, or whatfoever enterprife thou doft undertake, crave without ceafing my affiftance by prayer, and wait before the gates of my mercy. Thy prayers fhall never return from me void and fruitlefs, although thou think thou haft received nothing; for it is often more profitable for thee to pray humbly and earneftly than to receive and obtain benefits. It is often more gainful

for thee to truſt in me, and expect my leiſure, than fenſibly to feel or poſſeſs my conſolation. Wherefore be thou patient, and long-ſuffering, and increaſe in all good exerciſes, and in the love of all that is good; between falling and riſing, ever expect thou my grace and protection. Neither ſeek to fly or to run away from the battle, until all the fight be fully ended, and the time be come for thee to receive a glorious reward for thy painful travail.

14. And becauſe thou mayeſt be the rather encouraged to proceed in this labour, aſſure thyſelf that, even in this life, thy enemies ſhall be daily diminiſhed, and their forces that aſſault thee continually weakened, and thyſelf by my grace, and uſe of fighting, wonderfully ſtrengthened; inſomuch as that which at the firſt thou couldſt ſcarcely ſcrape out with a file of iron, thou ſhalt come in time to drive away with a blaſt of wind.

15. Moreover, whenſoever thou chanceſt to fall, take this for a general rule, though thou falleſt never ſo often, and offendeſt never ſo greatly, yet preſently without any

delay come unto me, lamenting thy fault and bewail it with me, lying proſtrate at my feet, and riſe again with me, leaning thyſelf upon me; that is, repoſe thy confidence in my power, reſolving firmly to amend, and never to offend in it again. I know man's weakneſs in general, I know alſo thine in particular, and how apt man is of his own frailty to fall, and how it proceedeth from the malice of the devil for a man to be unwilling to ſtand, or unwilling to riſe again after he is fallen. Which thing cannot only be by no means excuſed, but alſo receiveth without my mercy a heavier damnation. I require nothing of thee but a good will, and nothing is in my eyes more precious than the ſame.

16. Wherefore, if thou wanteſt force, ability, or time to do good works, be not diſmayed, for thy good will doth fully content me. Retain ever within thyſelf a good will, for by it thou mayeſt ſatisfy for all thy defeɛts, and repair all thy faults, although thou art able to do nothing beſides. When thou thinkeſt me fartheſt from thee, then am I neareſt unto thee. Therefore,

my Daughter, as soon as thou shalt find that thou haſt offended, condemn thyſelf, and preſently running unto me, confeſs thyſelf guilty, and make complaint againſt thyſelf unto me. Thou canſt not no sooner be repentant, than I have granted thee my pardon; neither canſt thou sooner aſk forgiveneſs, than I have quite remitted and forgiven all.

17. Wherefore, then, O my Spouſe, doſt thou ſtay from returning unto me? Thy ſafety is not procured in flying from me, but in flying unto me. In whatſoever thou ſeeſt that thou haſt moſt offended, where thou findeſt that thou haſt ofteneſt fallen, to conclude, where thou perceiveſt that thou haſt moſt declined from virtue, there cry ofteneſt unto me, there ſigh unto me with more frequent groans, and deſire, with all fervency at my hands, both pardon for thy ſins and the protection of my grace.

18. Be not wearied with temptations, but always reſiſt them as much as thou canſt; neither yield thyſelf as vanquiſhed by them, or as a priſoner unto them. As long as thou reſiſteſt thou art never overcome. For

To the Faithful Soul.

whatſoever thou feeleſt, and art enforced to ſuffer (as long as thou ſuffereſt it againſt thy will, and refiſting it as I told thee before), I will never impute it to thee as a fault, becauſe I require not an account at thy hands of that thou feeleſt, but of that to which thou confenteſt. To feel motions of ſin is ingrafted, as it were, in thy fleſh; but to confent unto it reſteth in thy own choice. There may be a certain kind of violence offered to the fleſh and fenſes, but the will can never be compelled.

19. There are two things in temptation: one, the matter whereunto thou art tempted, and that is a ſin, and imperfections; theſe thou muſt never confent unto, neither yet yield thyſelf in any fort unto them, but refiſt them with all thy might. The other is, that labour and diſtreſs which thou doſt endure in refiſting them; and this thou muſt patiently abide and yield unto, as long as it is my pleaſure that thou ſhalt be tempted. For thou oughteſt not to refiſt me, but to ſubject thyſelf wholly unto my will, and to refiſt thoſe motions which thou art ſtirred

unto by the means of temptation, that thou mayeſt continue ſtill in my favour, receive my grace, and be partaker of my conſolation.

20. But I know what thou wilt ſay, for I am not ignorant of thoſe things which thou doſt ſuffer, and wherewith thy heart is afflicted. I will tell thee them, therefore, ſince thou art aſhamed to tell them thyſelf, that by it thou mayeſt be the better aſſured to receive remedy and conſolation for them at my hands. The temptation of thy fleſh doth aſſault thee, not only every day, but every moment. To reſiſt this continually is troubleſome and grievous, and to eſcape it without fighting is impoſſible. To fight long, and not to be wounded, is, in thy judgment, not only hard but miraculous. He that is thy enemy is very familiar with thee; thou carrieſt him about with thee in every place; thou art not permitted to deſtroy him, but thou art enforced to nouriſh him. His weapons are many, his manner of fight divers, and his aſſaults very violent, as the fiery heats, the fervent motions, the delightful allurements, the

To the Faithful Soul. 55

terrible perturbations, the cruel onsets, the sweet pleasures of all kinds of lust and concupiscence, and many such other which some men do feel raging in their flesh like certain furies of hell. Now the strong impressions and delectations of them being in a manner violent, and joined with these fancies, are almost sufficient to vanquish all thy senses.

21. Moreover, the instability and inconstancy of some men's hearts are so great, that even in the very moment wherein they prepare themselves to resist these temptations, they are presently, as it were, fallen beside themselves, and clean forgetting that which they had determined, they begin to think of that which they did refuse to think of before. Now, who amongst these dangers (sayest thou) can escape safe? Who can fly away from sin unwounded? Only a good and humble will, for to it there can no violence be offered. For whatsoever thou thinkest, chastity is not polluted with it, but with the consent of thy mind; that is, whatsoever thou feelest in thy flesh shall not be imputed to thee for sin, if thy mind consent

not thereunto; for whatsoever is sin, must be voluntary, and as long as it is not voluntary, it is not sin.

22. Therefore, with how great temptations soever thou art oppressed—nay, though thy flesh do seem to be overwhelmed with them, and thy senses as prisoners unto them, yet whatsoever thou feelest delightful to thy flesh, keep thy mind free (that is, thy reasonable will), and then nothing can hurt thee. Cry out with the detestation of thy soul against them, and with a voice that doth abhor them, *Fye, fye, I will not, I will not.* Turn unto me with all the force thou art able, and repeat often this short sentence: *O, my God, help me; O, merciful Jesus, I will not yield unto them, help me.*

23. Moreover, though most loathsome and horrible temptations do creep into thy mind, yet for all that be thou not dismayed; as they creeped in so let them creep out, and by that gate wherein they did enter let them depart; and let them not only out themselves, but carry out with them anything that is naught and unclean within thee, that they may leave thy house

ſwept and cleanſed. And this thou mayeſt eaſily do, if thou wilt enter into a deep conſideration to know thyſelf, and call upon me only with a firm confidence, and with a great humility; neither ſeeking to ſpare thyſelf, nor ceaſing to perſecute thine enemies. For it is a moſt preſent remedy againſt all inclinations, to remember as ſoon as ever thou ſhalt find an evil inclination in thy mind how thou art nothing, and haſt nothing of thyſelf but by my grace only, and how impoſſible it is for thee, with any ability of thine own, to reſiſt theſe motions. Therefore, preſently fly unto me with all thy heart, and ſeek aid and protection from my wounds which I ſuffered for thy ſake, at the ſight whereof the ancient enemy of mankind doth yet quake and tremble.

24. Believe me (my Daughter) although thou be haunted as much as is poſſible for thee with carnal thoughts, ſenſual motions, violent cogitations, and imaginations, and although thou feel in this behalf as much as may be deviſed, yet as long as reaſon hath the upper-hand, and doth gainſay

them, and as long as thy reasonable and deliberate will doth not make choice of them, thou hast neither lost charity nor my grace. This distress which thou dost sustain, and these straits, whereinto thy heart is driven by the means of this conflict, may be a plain argument unto thee, that thou hast not consented unto them, and so consequently a great comfort to thy mind. For if thou hadst consented unto them, that is, if thou hadst willingly felt those things which thou didst feel, if thou hadst willingly retained those cogitations which did enter into thy mind, thou shouldst not then have felt this distress, this combat, and sharp conflict, but rather all peace and tranquillity in thy soul.

25. Receive a similitude (O my Daughter) at my hands for thy comfort. If any man in fight hand to hand be overcome, vanquished, bound, yea, and beaten, and although he be so straitly holden, as he hath not ability to use his own limbs; yet, if he yield not himself as a prisoner and vanquished, but resisteth with as much force as he is able, and consenteth not to this his

captivity, he can never be said to be conquered or overcome. In like manner, thou shalt never be judged of me to be overcome, whether thou be tempted of the flesh or the devil, except thou consent with thy mind, and ceasest to resist them. Thou must feel many things, which thou oughtest not to consent unto, that is, which thou oughtest not to feel with thy good will, and with a certain delight.

26. But thou wilt say, it is very painful to be in continual fight; it is painful to renounce those things which thou covetest; it is painful not to think of those things wherein thou delightest; it is painful to persecute those things which thou lovest. O my Daughter, thou dost consist of two parts, that is, of the flesh, and of the spirit, and therefore thy desires are divers; and those things which delight the flesh are painful to the spirit. If it seem painful to the flesh to offer violence to itself, if it cannot hate itself, let the spirit reign, let the spirit have the royal sovereignty and imperial authority in thee, and she will not think it any pain to bring her enemy, that

is, the flesh, under her yoke and subjection. That which seemeth at the first heavy, and almost intolerable, by continual use of fighting cometh to be light, and may well be endured; for the oftener that thou resisteth thy enemy, thou art the stronger, and he the weaker. For dost thou not know that the kingdom of heaven suffereth violence, and that the violent bear it away? Fight, therefore, manfully: the oftener and the more stoutly that thou dost do it, the more easy shalt thou ever find it.

27. Remember also that, as the temptations shall end so the fight shall not always continue, and that an eternal crown of glory, which is due to the conqueror, doth remain for thee. The sharper thy fight is, the more glorious thy crown of victory shall be. And, therefore, if thou overcomest, being tempted, thou shalt have a double reward; whereas, if thou hadst never been tempted, thou shouldst have received but a single. Moreover, the fiercer that thou art assaulted with the temptation of sin, the clearer shalt thou be purged from thy sins, if thou dost not consent unto it. And

although in this conflict, especially when a heavy temptation doth furiously rage in thy flesh, there are many venial sins wont to be committed (which are given as light wounds to those that fight), yet notwithstanding, that pain which is endured by continuing still in fight, and by resisting of mortal sins, doth on the contrary part take away all that pain, which the venial sins do deserve.

28. Besides, that charity wherewith thou, fighting for my sake, dost avoid mortal wounds, and takest great pain in striving for virtue, doth not only heal thy lesser wounds, but also doth turn them to thy greater glory and reward, if thou shalt perfectly overcome these temptations as the scars of a soldier's wounds, which he received by fighting manfully in a most fierce battle, are shewed after the victory to his great honour; and the sharper the battle was, the greater is his glory. Fear not, therefore, my Daughter, if thou art to fight long, or if thy temptation do continue strong, if thou canst not prevail so far over thy sensuality as to make it in all things

subject to thy reason, yet always resist it, never give it place, never grant it peace nor quietness. Thy battle against it, the conflict which thou didst endure in resisting of it, I will esteem as a victory and conquest over it.

29. For it is not only good to overcome evil, but with all thy might to resist evil; yea, it is sometimes more honourable and profitable for thee, by continuing in fight, to sustain longer the assaults of thine enemy and the labour of the conflict, than quickly to have vanquished him, especially when it is done by my providence (which disposeth of all, ever for the best, towards those that love me), and not by thy own sloth or negligence. For I, who am a most upright and wise judge, do mark the travail and force of every one of my soldiers, and do more esteem in them their will than their ability; because to be able to conquer proceedeth of my gift, but to be willing to conquer resteth in their own choice; and yet not that neither without my grace.

30. Wherefore, although my grace must of

necessity assist you in both, yet it resteth more in your own choice to be willing to do well than to be able to do well; which I confidering (O my Daughter) do better allow in thee a will to do much than ability to perform much. It is also both meet, and agreeth with justice, that the longer thou fightest, and the more pain thou takest, thou shouldst receive the larger reward; and not only a reward in the life to come, but even here grace for grace; that is, for every good work which you do by my grace, you shall receive a reward, and some benefit or other by my gracious favour in this present world.

Chap. VII.

How we must Fly the Occasions of Temptation.

TAKE a special care that thou art not an occasion of thine own temptation or destruction, in giving thine enemy, by thine own fault, opportunity to assault thee, and ability to overthrow thee. For avoiding whereof, fly provocations of temptation, restrain thy senses from wandering, shew the familiarity and private friendship both of men and women, whereby sometimes the devil doth find an opportunity to tempt thee under the colour of devotion or spiritual love. For these things, for the most part, do leave behind them grievous temptations, of doubtful suspicions, perturbations, distractions, or else some scandals of violent love and affection.

2. If thy enemy which sought to take thy life stood at thy door, wouldst thou suffer him to come in? How quickly and carefully wouldst thou shut and bar the gates against him! Now, these carnal and vicious imaginations, cogitations, and affections do seek by all means to enter thy heart, and to destroy the life of thy soul—wilt thou then let them come in? Do not suffer them to enter; drive me not away, but keep them out of thy house by force, and with a horrible detestation of them. Turn thy heart unto me, and, if thou feel anything in thy flesh, turn thy heart away from it.

3. Punish thy flesh when it waxeth proud or wanton, with abstinence and temperance, both in meat and drink. Cut off all access of persons, all haunting of places, and all taking of any occasions whereby thou perceivest thyself to be tempted. And beware, above all things, that thou yield not thine own members so far to iniquity, as that the devil do make them instruments of iniquity, and so by thy negligence take opportunity to wound thee with thine own weapons. And therefore correct the pride of thy flesh with such strait discipline, and bridle it with so great modesty and bashfulness, that even for very fervent love of shame and chastity, thou mayest scarce presume to see or touch any naked part of thy hands or feet.

4. And for all unclean cogitation, which shall chance to be still importunate upon thee, drive them out, as it were one nail with another, by some godly meditation, and imprinting in thy mind some holy impression of my life and passion. For, to think of my wounds and passion doth ever yield, without all doubt, a continual and

wonderful increase of virtue. For if I have infused into herbs, stones, and roots, rare virtues to expel many diseases of the body, how unspeakable and how effectual is the virtue I have given to my wounds and passion for expelling of spiritual diseases, and both curing and sanctifying of the soul.

Chap. VIII.

When Spiritual Temptations are to be Conquered.

IF filthy and unclean thoughts, as it often happeneth, do at some time enter into thy mind against me and my saints; or else that thou be tempted with blasphemy and rebellious cogitations; let it never henceforth trouble thee, nor yet make thee faint-hearted; neither be thou perplexed in thy mind with thinking how to make thy confession of any such matter, as long as thou dost not with advised and deliberate consent yield unto them. For they carry with them more grief than delight, and thou rather suffereft,

than doeſt thoſe things, being for that time altogether in paſſion and nothing in action.

2. Wherefore, he that carrieth a pure mind need not either to fear them or confeſs them. For although a godly mind may ſeem to be by this means a little polluted, yet is it not defiled by her own fault and negligence. And, therefore, ſuch things as theſe, which procure great heavineſs to a devout heart, and my Spouſe (becauſe ſhe is enforced to feel within herſelf, and to be turmoiled with ſuch filthy imaginations and cogitations againſt me, as thoſe who are the greateſt ſinners do abhor) are rather an affliction and purgation unto her, than any defiling or pollution of her. For the Devil, whilſt he feeth thee withdrawn from all other things whatſoever, and only to thirſt after me, doth endeavour to trouble this quiet peace of thine, and to hinder and to keep thee from being united unto me, by theſe fancies which ſeem both odious and horrible.

3. Wherefore the more holy that the day is, the more earneſtly thou doſt bend thyſelf to the exerciſe of divine actions, the more thou doſt ſeek to lift up thy heart, and

the more vehemently that thou doſt ſtrive to unite thyſelf wholly unto me; the more violently, wickedly and importunately do theſe imaginations aſſault thee, being ſtirred up either by the Devil or by ſome timorous fearfulneſs of thy own; becauſe as ſoon as thy ſoul doth begin to abhor and fear a thing, ſhe doth preſently feel and find the ſame which ſhe feareth, or for which ſhe is afraid. For fear and faint-heartedneſs do quicklieſt thruſt into a man's mind that imagination which is feared. And the Devil alſo doth raiſe theſe perturbations and motions within thy ſoul, that whilſt thou art buſied in ſeeking to reſiſt them, thou mayeſt be withholden from feeling the ſweet taſte of my charity; or elſe, being too much diſmayed with them, thou mayeſt be afraid, and not preſume to approach unto me.

4. The Devil doth this becauſe he delighteth to entangle thy mind with ſcruples and perturbations, and by them to hinder the ſabbath of thy quiet reſt. But do not regard them, do not fear them, do not anſwer them, do not reſiſt them, do not ob-

serve them, but go forward in thy godly devotion and holy exercife, as though thou felt nothing, and as though thy mind were troubled with nothing; and pafs over all thefe filthy cogitations, as the barking of a cur, or the hiffing of a goofe, to which a man will difdain to make an anfwer, and will not ftay either to contend or ftrive with them, but only pafs by them, and laugh at them. In doing thus, thou fhalt eafily avoid and quickly forget them. But if thou feekeft to refift them, to difpute with them, to fear them, to regard them, to hearken unto them, and to remove them; thou fhalt ftill the more deeply imprint them in thy mind, and the more dangeroufly entangle thyfelf with great perturbation. For thefe temptations are not vanquifhed by fighting with them, but by contemning of them.

5. Take heed alfo, that no temptation overcome thee by importunity, and by making thee weary to refift it, for this is an ufual practice of the Devil to vex fome with fo long and troublefome a temptation, that he overcometh thofe by trying them with

that wicked device of his, whom he could neither deceive by subtlety, nor entice by pleasure. Wherefore thou hast need to be long-suffering, constant, and patient; and as thou oughtest to detest those wicked cogitations, which are thrown into thy mind by the craft of the Devil against my honour, and are brought in of purpose to seduce thee; so thou mayest in no sort either mislike or seek to shun that affliction which I send unto thee, nor those heavy and troublesome burthens which thou feelest by my will and providence laid upon thee; nor yet that pain which thou takest in any conflict, when thou strivest to resist vice and iniquity, but thou oughtest for my sake to bear them patiently, and without any grudging.

6. Of this also I am to warn thee, that if thou be tempted with any carnal vices, as gluttony and concupiscence, thou mayest more easily vanquish them by flying them, than by fighting with them; but on the contrary part, all spiritual vices are ever overcome, not by slightly passing over them, but by staying with good considera-tion upon them, and doing the contrary of

that to which they allure thee. For the temptation of pride is neither any whit diminifhed, nor yet vanquifhed, by flying all occafions that may any way move thee to humble thyfelf, that is, by flying all the means that may procure humility in thee, in hope by that courfe to abate the force, and avoid the motions of that temptation. But if thou wilt overcome it, ftay advifedly upon it, and enforce thyfelf to do thofe things that may humble thee.

7. Thou fhalt after the fame fort overcome envy, if prefently and violently, as it were in fpite of her, thou doft thofe things from which fhe diffuadeth thee; that is, if thou fpeakeft to thy brother, if thou feekeft to do him fervice, if thou doft humble thyfelf unto him. In like manner alfo, thou fhalt never conquer flothfulnefs flying all travail, or by negleƈting the divine honouring and ferving of me, and by feeking to withdraw thyfelf, that thou mighteft not be commanded to labour, and take pains; but by enforcing thyfelf with all thy might, and by applying wholly of thy mind to praƈtife and perform devout and virtuous exercifes.

Chap. IX.

How we ought to take heed of Envy.

BEWARE of envy as much as possibly thou canst, that by it thou be not brought to mislike with any man, to speak in derogation of him, to prefer thyself before him, to molest and vex him, and to be also thyself vexed (if he be preferred before thee) with his virtue, with his honour, with his commendation, or with his spiritual profit.

2. To overcome this temptation, be more courteous and lowly unto him, my daughter, than to another; speak nothing of him thyself, nor hear him spoken of in his absence; neither yet let anything proceed from thee in word, deed, or show, that may seem to favour of envy, or to spring from that venomous root.

Chap. X.

How we muſt fly Singularity.

SHEW not in thy converſation with others any ſad or unquiet countenance, but a courteous kind of behaviour, left thy converſation ſeem troubleſome or unpleaſant unto them.

2. Beware of being ſingular, and uſing any particular faſhion by thyſelf, different from the reſt, in any unneceſſary ceremony, act, or ſhew of devotion, when thou art in other men's company; and as for thoſe points which are profitable for thy ſoul, which thy calling and Chriſtian profeſſion requireth at thy hands, and which are neceſſary, either for obtaining of virtue or avoiding of ſins, fear not to be ſingular in them; conform not thyſelf in thoſe to other men's fancies, if they be careleſs of their own ſalvation; but rather reſolve for the benefit of thine own ſoul, the obtaining

of virtue, and the fulfilling of my good pleaſure, conſtantly, humbly, and patiently to bear all their deriſions, and perſecutions for the ſame.

Chap. XI.

Of the Honour, Reverence, and Worſhip which we ought to exhibit unto the Mother of God.

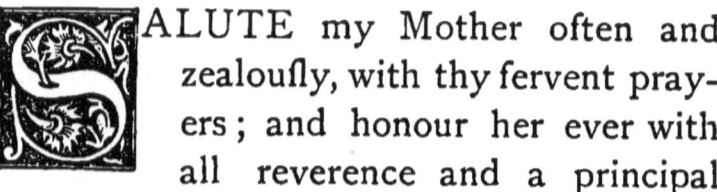ALUTE my Mother often and zealouſly, with thy fervent prayers; and honour her ever with all reverence and a principal devotion, by ſeeking diligently to imitate both her life and her virtue. For I gave her to this world as a perfect example of ſanctity, innocency, and purity, as a ſingular patroneſs, and moſt ſafe refuge for all my ſervants, and as a ſanctuary of ſo great freedom to all thoſe which are in miſery and tribulation; as no man might have cauſe to miſlike it, no man might fear to take it, nor yet be in doubt to approach unto it.

2. And to that end I made her fo meek, fo virtuous, fo merciful, fo gentle, and fo gracious, as fhe might defpife no man, deny her aid to no man, but ever lay open her bofom of pity before all men, and not to fuffer any man to depart from her fad, nor without confolation. I made her alfo gracious, amiable, worthy to be beloved, and after a wonderful fort moft fweet and delightful to thofe who otherwife were defperate and obftinate finners, that fhe might be a meet bait for my hook to catch all fouls, but fpecially fuch as could by no other means be taken. For thofe heinous finners who break out of all other nets, and for whom I cannot find an apt courfe by any other way to draw them unto me, I ufe to catch by her means; that is, by the veneration of her, and their devotion towards her, whom I make to tafte moft fweet in their hearts, and excite thofe who are hard-hearted towards me, to perform good works unto her,—that is, acts of veneration, devotion, confidence, and invocation, and by this means I make them veffels fitter and worthier to receive my grace, and

greater illumination from me, until they attain to a more reformed and, for the moſt part, a moſt holy courſe of life.

3. Recommend thyſelf daily, therefore, unto her protection, that by her help thou mayeſt receive greater grace and favour at my hands. For I committed unto her cuſtody the whole treaſure of my grace and mercy, to be diſtributed and beſtowed, when I recommended unto her all my ſons, in the person of *John*, as her ſons, but ſpecially ſinners, for whom I did at that preſent ſuffer. This ſhe knoweth very well, and therefore is ſo careful and diligent to diſcharge the office ſhe received from me, as ſhe ſuffereth none of thoſe (as far as lieth in her power) which were committed unto her, and principally ſuch as call upon her, to periſh, but refereth them unto me, both with her earneſt prayers and by all the other means ſhe is able, that they may be reconciled unto me, and received again into my favour.

4. Doſt thou think then, my daughter, that I could have choſen any more fit and more meet for this buſineſs? Could I

have found any that had been fo apt and able every way to have difcharged this office? Doft thou think that fuch as are forrowful, defolate, and overwhelmed with their fins, will defire any other mediator for them unto me, who may fue more faithfully in their behalf, and be more gracioufly inclined to receive them, and more ready to bring them unto me, than this woman, this moft humble, moft pitiful, moft meek, and moft loving Virgin, abounding with all fweetnefs and mercy, being moft mighty of herfelf to relieve finners, and moft acceptable unto me becaufe fhe is my mother, yea, even his mother whofe wrath is to be pacified and appeafed towards them?

5. Alas, how far do they err; how great a burthen of wilful obftinacy and perdition do they heap upon their own backs, who do mutter and murmur againft this holy Virgin, who hath the cuftody and beftowing of my graces, and will not acknowledge her for an advocate unto me as I am to my Father? Doft thou think that they can by any means throw themfelves more head-

long into the bottomless pit of hell, than by making her their enemy (for whose sake I have so often spared the world, and so often forborne to pour my wrath upon men), that when there is none to be a mediator for them, or to withhold my hand which is ready bent to punish them, I may, without any let or impediment, strike them as often and as much as I will? But what greater pain or punishment can I lay upon these men, than not to chasten them temporally here as children, but to deliver them over as my enemies into a reprobate sense, that they being blind may not see into what danger they run, until they find themselves drowned in perpetual darkness, and overwhelmed with eternal destruction?

6. I do use these exhortations unto thee, as unto my Spouse, of mere love and good-will, that being instructed by my spirit, thou mayest not decline either in this or in any other matter whatsoever, be it never so small, from the decrees and resolution of doctrine, which my holy Catholic Church hath determined and resolved upon; nor yet suffer thyself to be deceived

by that wicked and malignant fpirit of theirs, which pretend in fhow to be followers of the Gofpel, and are in truth nothing less.

Chap. XII.

Of Senfible Devotion.

IF thou findeft not fenfible devotion, be not therefore grieved nor dejected in thy foul, but do with a ftout and conftant mind (although thou feeleft it dry and barren) whatfoever thou knoweft to be for my honour, and as much as thou art able to perform in that behalf. There are many who, fhedding tears, do feem to have fome fpiritual devotion and fweet tafte in their foul, and yet their life is never a whit the holier, nor themfelves at that time free from mortal fin, but it proceedeth from a certain tendernefs of their heart, as is often feen in women, and alfo in men, that are by nature paffionate and full of compaffion. Have no confidence, therefore, in that devo-

tion which doth not better and amend thy life.

2. Thou shalt see some weep often, and be sorrowful for the death of a valiant captain, whose worthy and famous acts they have only read, though he were a Gentile or a Pagan. They will weep also sometimes if they read of a heavy parting or a pitiful death of two constant lovers. What wonder is it, then, if they weep at my most holy and devout service, by seeing many pathetical things done in the worshipping of me, or by taking compassion of those things which I did suffer for them, or by rejoicing at that honour which is done unto me, and yet these tears proceed from a natural passion of their heart, without any virtuous intention or profitable fruit to their souls, as long as they do not my will, and fulfil my commandment? If, therefore, thou findest thy heart hardened and barren, without such devotion, endeavour thou to have another kind of devotion, which is a true, perfect, and ready will, with a determined resolution to do all those things which may honour and please me.

3. Moreover, for the want of the other, that is, fenfible devotion, feek out the true caufe and reafon, left perhaps thou haft loft that fweet tafte in thy foul, by fome diffolute motion, by lightnefs, by inordinate love, or unmeafureable joy, or left thou haft been too much bufied with earthly cogitations, or elfe, left thou haft polluted thy foul with the fpots of pride, or haft fought to pleafe thine own fancy, or for fome fuch other vice and offence. In which cafe thou oughteft to be rather grieved for the caufe of this barrennefs of thy foul, that is, thou oughteft to be more forry for the fault which thou haft committed, than for the devotion which thou haft loft. Endeavour to cleave unto me, with a good and pure will, fevered from earthly affections, and with a naked and fimple underftanding, far from conceiving of needlefs or unprofitable matters, and omit to do no good thing that either thou wert accuftomed to ufe before, or that may tend to my honour, but remain patient with renouncing of thine own appetite, and expect my pleafure, with refigning of thyfelf wholly unto the fame.

4. And although somewhat, at some times, do suddenly break out of thy sensual disposition and outward man, or remain boiling in thy mind, which is not convenient for thy profession, or else, if there arise any perturbations in thee, if thou sufferest any distress, if thou be oppressed with the temptations of heaviness in thy soul, resisting or murmuring, take special care, that at the least thy inward and reasonable man, being subject unto me, continue settled in all tranquillity, in loving of my commandments, and in labouring to fulfil them.

Chap. XIII.

How we must Prepare Ourselves when we come to Receive the Blessed Sacrament.

TO speak somewhat by the way of that preparation which thou oughtest to make when thou comest to receive the Blessed Sacrament of my precious body, I am first to admonish thee that thou shouldst not be discouraged, although thou dost not sensibly feel devotion in thee, yea, although thou findest thyself troubled with horrible temptations, and assaulted with some odious imaginations, which do invade thy mind. For this sensible devotion of thy soul is not so necessary, but rather that reasonable devotion of thy will, whereby thou dost believe well of my Sacrament, and whereby (notwithstanding these blasphemous thoughts which do assail and almost overwhelm thee) thou mayest be moved to do all honour and reverence to my Sacrament, although it be against thine appetite, contrary to thy liking, and repugnant to the sense or opinion of thine own heart.

2. And lastly, that thou mayest by this enforcing of thyself against thy carnal desire, find thy will ready, and prepared with all obedience to honour me, to give me thanks, to resign thyself wholly unto me, and to subject thy mind so far to my liking, as that it may be best contented with that which agreeth most with my pleasure. If thou hast this devotion, my Daughter, which thy reasonable will may easily command

and procure in thee, that is, if thou be forry that thou haft ever offended me, and determined never to offend me again, but to endeavour as much as poffibly thou canft in all things to obey my will, thou mayeft come boldly unto this Sacrament, thou mayeft enter fecurely into my prefence; for neither reafonable nor fenfible devotion, neither virtue, nor yet my grace is obtained by flying from me, but by approaching near unto me.

3. Therefore, the fadder and the more defolate that thou findeft thyfelf, yea, although it be at that time when thou art going to confeffion, or to receive my Bleffed Body, the more earneftly and vehemently excite and enforce thyfelf to proceed in thy good purpofe, that thou mayeft be made ftronger in grace, more conftant in goodnefs, and more fervent in love towards me. Provided always, that thou carrieft with thee a pure intention and a good will, as I faid before.

4. Neither let it trouble thee if, even in coming to receive this Bleffed Sacrament, there doth enter fome horror and terror into

To the Faithful Soul. 85

thy foul, or if thou be fcarce able prefently to take and fwallow the Bleffed Hoft, or if thou find fome gallifh kind of bitternefs in thy tafte, for thefe are not certain figns that thou cameft unworthily to it ; but thou haft rather caufe to miftruft that fear, faint-heartednefs, and continual cuftom of trembling, have procured this imagination in thee, which is ftrongeft of all in women, and maketh thee to think that thou feeleft thofe things indeed, which either thou dreadeft to feel hereafter, or thou doft imagine that thou feeleft at that prefent. But if thou couldft clean remove this faint-heartednefs, and fearful imaginations of thine, thou fhouldft with it alfo clean expel this difficulty and diftrefs which thou findeft in thy mind. For albeit I could deliver thee from all thefe perturbations, yet do I permit fome fuch diftrefs as thefe to affault thee and other of my fervants, becaufe I know it is the beft means either to keep all of you humble, or, by humbling of you, to deliver you from the fin of pride, which is in woman moft ufual.

5. Be therefore ftout, and carry a refolute

mind, that, shaking off all womanish fear or faint-heartedness, and purging it from those filthy cogitations which do enter into thee, by contemning of them and their persuasions, thou mayest with a quiet mind, and a pure conscience, wholly dedicated to my service, desire me, seek me, and receive me in the Blessed Sacrament, who am and will always remain unto thee (if the fault be not in thyself) a most gracious lover, a most gentle protector, a most merciful Redeemer, a most loving preserver, and a most faithful Saviour. But because thou mayest be inflamed with a greater reverence, love, and desire, towards this Blessed Sacrament, I assure thee that, without all doubt, my body is there sacramentally delivered unto thee, to be received under the form of bread.

6. Wherefore, seeing it is the same body, which I now carry glorified in heaven; seeing it is no other, nor any like unto it, but even the very same; and seeing I carry not a body which is dead nor without blood, it followeth of necessity that, together in the same body, there must be also contained

my foul, my blood, my graces, and my virtues; to all which, fince the Word is united—that is, one perfon in Trinity—the two other perfons cannot be divided, but are infeparably united, it muft alfo follow, that the whole Trinity is prefent in this Sacrament, as truly and as verily as they are in heaven, though in another kind, that is, under a facramental form. The fame opinion thou muft in like fort have of the Chalice, the new Teftament in my Blood; confider, therefore, now with thyfelf with how great willingnefs and defire thou oughteft to come unto this Sacrament, feeing that thou haft in it true falvation, and that thou haft me really and perfectly there, who am the author of all thy happinefs.

7. And becaufe I would not have thee drawn from it with too much timoroufnefs of thy confcience, or with too great a fear of the reverence and majefty thereof, I have commanded thee to come unto it, and to receive it for a commemoration of me, affuring thee that my delight is to be with the children of men, and that I do much

rejoice when I may do any of you good, and to knock at the gate of your hearts, that being entered in, I may sup with you, and both feed and refresh your hungry spirit with myself. And to what other end do I all these things, but only to procure you to have a hope and confidence in me, with a love and desire to come unto me, and not to withdraw yourselves from so profitable and necessary a Sacrament, or to deprive your souls of that infinite and inestimable fruit, which you shall receive thereby, for fear of being made unworthy by these temptations which you feel against your will, and therefore are not by them polluted with any sin.

Chap. XIV.

Of Discretion.

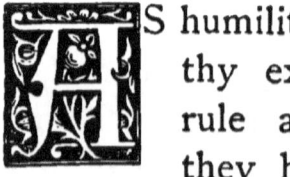S humility must be the guide of all thy exercises, so let discretion rule and moderate them, lest they hurt thee, or make thee unable to do thy duty, or lest the greater benefits and better exercises of thy soul be

To the Faithful Soul. 89

hindered by the outward exercifes of thy body, which are not fo good, nor fo profitable; and to conclude, left by exercifing of any virtuous act thou doft fomewhat offend in breach of charity.

2. Have confideration alfo of the infirmity of thy body, and take care that thou confume not thy ftrength, if thou be weak, and govern all thy intents, ftudies, and exercifes by the direction of fuch as fear me, or are thy fuperiors, leaving or leffening them, increafing or moderating them, according to their will and counfel. Wherefore, if thy fuperior, who hath the charge of thy foul, as being my deputy, and difcharging of that office in my ftead towards thee, forbid thee to faft, or any other thing that is not in itfelf fin, obey him, believing that he, knowing thy ability every way, doth advife and command thee to that which may be fitteft and moft neceffary for thy falvation.

3. And therefore, my Daughter, if thou art bidden to eat eight times in a day, thou fhalt not in obeying it offend me. Neverthelefs, retain ftill a will to faft, when thou haft liberty to ufe thine own difcretion.

But if for obedience' sake thou eat, thou shalt by eating receive of me a double reward, whereas otherwise by fasting thou shouldst have had but only a single. For thy good will to fast, and the fruit of thy good will is not lost, if thou eatest to shew only thy obedience; but being done for obedience' sake, it is, together with obedience, crowned and rewarded in thee. In like sort it is in all other things which thou desirest of thine own will to do, and art enforced to omit only to shew thy obedience.

4. Seek daily, desire earnestly, study continually, to set forth and advance my glory as much as thou art able, and wheresoever thou canst, and to fulfil my will both in thyself and in all others. Neglect to do no good work that thou hast ability to perform, but go forward in goodness every day, and strive always to increase in virtue; but neither glory nor rejoice in thyself for all the travail, study, and exercise which thou usest in doing of good works; neither be thou comforted with it, as though thou hadst anything, wert anything, or able to

To the Faithful Soul. 91

do anything of thyfelf, but fix thine eyes ever upon thine own bafenefs and imbecility, remembering that thou art merely nothing but of my grace, and therefore afcribe all the good thou doft to me only.

5. There are fome who are not contented with that correction of their flefh which I do lay upon them, but do torment their bodies with indifcreet abftinence and immoderate afflictions, and make themfelves by that means not only unapt and unable to obey me, to follow my fteps, and to endure the conflicts of this fpiritual battle; but alfo being tired and confumed in their natural ftrength by this indifcreet dealing, are enforced to leave thofe exercifes which they were wont to ufe before, and to take more care of their flefh than is requifite or convenient, for repairing of that which was decayed by their own folly. Wherefore, moderate thou thy exercifes and labours, according to the proportion of thy force and ability, left thou doft furcharge and overthrow thyfelf; and fail not by good means to nourifh thy body: it is my will that thou fhouldft comfort nature, and re-

pair from time to time thine infirmity; not with an extraordinary care or delight, but for the refreshing of nature, as I said before.

6. And for the better enabling of thy body to do me service, to yield thyself a fit instrument of my grace, to fulfil my will, to follow my commandment, and to do those works which are most acceptable in my sight; being always as ready, if it be my pleasure, to suffer poverty, as to enjoy riches, and as willing to be sick as to be whole. But when thou shalt not be compelled by discretion to nourish thy body for infirmity of nature, take heed lest by impatience or want of devotion, or of an insatiable desire to please thine own appetite, thou seekest evasions to escape, and deliver thyself from those adversities or troubles which I send thee. But remember to receive such crosses as are of my sending gladly, sustain them patiently, complain of them to nobody, bear them with long-suffering, and stay with all meekness, expecting of my pleasure.

7. Suffer me to deal with thee as I think fit, that by that tribulation which falleth

upon thee, my grace may work ſome good effect in thee. This is much better and more profitable for thee, than that which of thine own head thou layeſt upon thyſelf. For I would have thee to be fully perſuaded, my Daughter, that I never permit thee to ſuffer any tribulation but that it is for thy good, and for the purging and repairing of thy ſoul, which is weakened or impaired by ſin, if thou wouldſt believe me, and refer thyſelf wholly unto me, by bearing it with ſilence, and wait my leiſure by patient ſuffering thereof. For I will come at the laſt, who am never abſent from thee, but am always ready in all places to aſſiſt thee.

8. Beware, therefore, that thou doſt not deſpiſe thoſe afflictions which I do ſend and lay upon thee, for I will guide thee in them; rely upon me, truſting in my providence and love towards thee, and not in thine own will and ability. Be content that I and other men do afflict thee: in the meantime, do not thou perſecute thy fleſh, but thy faults, and endure with patience whatſoever ſhall happen unto thee.

Chap. XV.

How we ought in all Things to Conform Ourselves unto Christ.

 FAITHFUL Spouse ought to be so loving to her husband, as she should desire with all her heart ever to be with him, never without him, and at no time from him; she should wish to conform herself in all things unto her husband's mind, and be glad when she is in anything like unto him. After the same manner thou must behave thyself. Consider my life, my actions, and my virtues, whereby thou mayest learn what I love, and what doth please me in thee.

2. Now if thou wilt be a faithful spouse, O soul, thou oughtest to desire nothing so much as to please me, and to frame thyself in all things agreeable to my will. Wheresoever, therefore, that I go, desire to accompany me; whatsoever I do, study to imitate me; whatsoever I suffer, be ready to suffer with me; and if by any occasion thou feelest tribulation, rejoice in it, because by it thou art made like unto me.

3. Confider and recount with thyfelf every one of my virtues, or at leaft the principal, whereby thou mayeft ftir up a defire in thy mind to imitate and follow me. It fhall be an eafier labour for thee than to cut off, mortify, and rafe out all thofe things which are contrary and unlike to my courfe of life; that is, thy vices, thy wicked inclinations, and corrupt affections. And as I faid before, thou fhalt attain to fuch a habit of well-doing in time, by a ftudious will, a watchful care, and continual travail, that thou mayeft come hereafter to drive away that (as it were) with one blaft of wind, which thou canft now fcarce fcrape away with a file of iron.

Chap. XVI.

Of Poverty.

BEHOLD, therefore, firft my poverty, who when I was rich made myfelf poor for thy fake; how I came to mine own, and mine did not receive me; how I was very poor, and as a stranger and sojourner in a foreign land; how my mother being lodged in an inn, as a guest in a strange place, I was born in a stable before the mouths of beasts, which, by the heat of their breath, might defend me from the bitter cold, being laid upon hay in a manger; how I was redeemed with the sacrifice of poor innocents; how, being an infant, I was driven into banishment, brought up by the labour of my mother, and fed by alms at other folks' cost, having neither house nor lodging of mine own; how I watched often in the mountains; how I was despoiled of all my garments at the time of my passion, and died naked upon the Cross; being in so great want of all things, as I could not have a drop of water in my most extreme thirst, to refresh my dried tongue; lastly, how, after my death, I was buried in the grave that was made for another.

2. Moreover, how often dost thou think that I suffered in the whole course of my life, hunger, cold, thirst, and other vexations of my body? And as for corporal consolation (which most men do think very

neceſſary) I refuſed, and utterly rejected it, patiently enduring penury and poverty in all things. But thou, when thou haſt everything ready at hand that thou canſt deſire, thou doſt flatter thyſelf, and thinkeſt that thou liveſt in poverty, and doſt repine if thou canſt not have every other thing that thou wanteſt, although it be merely ſuperfluous, and more to pleaſe thy envious mind, than to ſerve thy neceſſary uſe.

3. Look, therefore, upon my poverty, and leave off being ſad, and ceaſe to be offended if thou feeſt any man preferred before thee, or endowed with greater abundance than thyſelf. Why art thou not rather grieved like a good emulatreſs, if thou ſee any one poorer than thyſelf, as S. Francis was? If thou perceiveſt any man (which opinion thou oughteſt to carry of all men) more agreeable to my life and poverty than thyſelf, this ſhould be a good kind of emulation, not to be grieved with other men's happineſs, or that they are better than thou art, but to be heartily forry becauſe thou art not good thyſelf,

and that it proceedeth of thine own fault and negligence.

4. Rejoice, therefore, and receive it for a special token of my grace, for an exceeding benefit, if I make thee more agreeable to myself than other men, by sending thee some grievous sickness, some extreme poverty, misery, misfortune, or contempt in this world. And if thou wantest necessary things, rejoice; if they are taken away, be glad, and complain of it to no man, but embrace with me the cross of poverty, being quiet and contented in thy mind, using silence, and utterly renouncing of thine own self. What doth it profit thee, my Daughter, if thou hast for my sake forsaken the world, her riches, her glory, and the comfort of thy friends, and art now troubled about a thing not worth a straw, or hast not yet abandoned all love for such vanities as are of no value, but art ready to fight, to be vexed, and to contend either for desire to attain them, or for fear to lose them, and art not afraid in this behalf to break peace and charity with thy neighbour?

5. Determine, therefore, now, and make a firm refolution from the bottom of thy heart, to contemn all things for the love of me, and be unwilling to poffefs anything, but even fuch as of neceffity thou art enforced to ufe, delighting in all poverty, contempt, and penury; that thou mayeft be worthy to enjoy me, who, as I am better and more profitable for thee than a thoufand worlds, fo ought I to be more efteemed, and more dearly beloved of thee, than all earthly things whatfoever. Why ftayeft thou, my Daughter? Be encouraged with my example, be enflamed with my love, and feek earneftly in everything that appertaineth to thyfelf, to live in all want and poverty.

6. Moreover, think other men worthy of my confolation, becaufe they are my faithful fervants, being far better than thyfelf, and not fo unthankful as thou art. And, therefore, being moved with charity, and, as it were, enforced with compaffion, fuffer no man to want anything that thou mayeft fupply, but help all men with thy travail, thy fervice, thy friendfhip, and by all the

other means that are within the compaſs of thine ability. Whatſoever thou haſt, think it to be other men's, that neither thou mayeſt love it when thou poſſeſſeſt it, nor be grieved when thou loſeſt it. Whatſoever thou doſt enjoy, think it is given thee for other men's uſe, and to ſerve their neceſſity.

Chap. XVII.

Of Humility.

DETEST and abhor with all thy heart the honour, glory, and favour of men, with all other flatteries and enticements of this deceitful world. Think no otherwiſe of thyſelf, but as a proud man, unthankful to me, ſpiteful againſt me, and, therefore (if I ſhould reward thee according to thy deſerts), worthy to be hated above all creatures, as one unworthy to be born by the earth, to receive breath by the air, or to be nouriſhed and ſerved by any of my creatures. Wherefore, aſk always at my hands mercy and grace, not relying upon any work or merit of thine own, but trufting altogether in that only work of redemption which I finifhed for thee, and that unfpeakable mercy which I fhewed towards thee. Defire of me, with tears and fighs, perfect humility, that by it thou mayeft delight to lie hidden and unknown, to be contemned, and held in no eftimation.

2. Endeavour, as much as thou canft, to love thofe things which are moft vile, and fhew greateft humility. Choofe, likewife, both to do and to have thofe things which are moft abject, and which other men do moft defpife, thinking thyfelf more bafe, and lefs worthy, than thofe things that are moft vile. Seek not to fet forth in thyfelf anything that may favour of eftimation, or glory, or that may fhew, as it were, any fingular gift in thee, except thou be enforced to it by neceffity, or of mere charity for the glory of God. Glory in nothing, neither yet boaft thyfelf of anything that is in thee. And if any man do offend or contemn thee, take heed thou be

not angry with him for it, neither ufe him with worfe countenance in fhew, nor bear him lefs good will in thy heart. But rather marvel that every creature doth not perfecute thee, to be revenged of the injury thou doft to me, who am Creator both of thee and all them, and whom, notwithftanding, thou art nothing at all afraid to offend.

Chap. XVIII.

How Humility is to be Obtained.

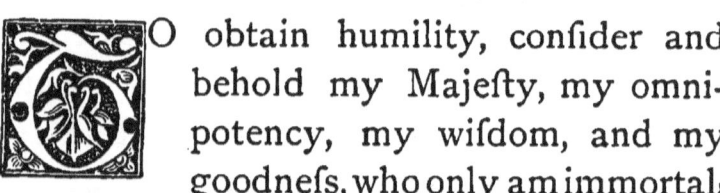O obtain humility, confider and behold my Majefty, my omnipotency, my wifdom, and my goodnefs, who only am immortal, only infinite, paffing all meafure, without all limitation or circumfcription, unfpeakable, incomprehenfible, from whom all creatures receive their being, and who am able with a beck, both to bring all creatures and the whole world unto nothing, and again prefently to reftore all things to their former courfe and order. Therefore, feeing

To the Faithful Soul.

I am every way of so great power, you may easily perceive that I created you, who are reasonable creatures, according to mine own image, not for necessity, or for any need that I had of you, but of my charity and goodness towards you, as persons upon whom I meant to bestow my benefits, and with whom I would impart my felicity.

2. From which grace, since you fell by sin, whereby you made yourselves, not only unworthy of eternal life, but justly deserved eternal fire, I being incarnate for your sakes suffered three-and-thirty years' hunger, thirst, cold, heat, miseries, labours, persecutions, contempts, reproaches, stripes, blows, wounds, griefs, torments, and lastly the Cross, and death itself; that I might deliver you from eternal death, which you had incurred by your own deserts, I lived, my Daughter, in the world not as a God, not as a mighty person, nor in a glorious shew, but as the poorest, vilest, basest, and most contemptible of all others; being subject to many torments and sundry reproaches, until at the last I was slain,

with a most shameful and ignominious death, which the world did think I had justly deserved, for they judged both my life and doctrine to be so detestable, as they thought it fit to root them both out of all men's memory, and to make them end with my death, whereat a great multitude of people being present, did triumph and rejoice.

3. Yet went I as gladly to suffer it as the hart doth to the fountains of water; nay, being made drunk with my love towards thee, I ran unto it and was never well until I had endured it. I spared not myself, neither fled I any labour, grief, pain, or torment whatsoever. I refused to do nothing that might be for thy profit; thou wert so dear and precious in my sight, that I did even long with a desire to deliver myself for thy sake, to be wounded in all parts, with sundry kinds of torments, and for thy sake also, at the last, to end my life with a shameful death. Moreover, because I did vehemently thirst after thy salvation, I desired to shed all my blood for thee, which I did in such plentiful sort, as I left

not one drop thereof remaining within my body.

4. But how doſt thou, O my Daughter, requite me now for all this? What doſt thou render again unto me in recompenſe of ſo great charity? Is it not even thou who, being unthankful unto me ſo many years, didſt deſpiſe me, didſt not regard my words, didſt loathe my ſervice, and didſt tranſgreſs my commandments? And yet ſhewing all reproach towards me, being moſt unclean and vile in my ſight; being altogether polluted with ſo many filthy abominations, thou doſt baniſh me from thee and thou doſt reject my inſpirations, thou committeſt fornication with my creatures, thou abuſeſt my gifts. Why doſt thou ſtill contemn and forſake me, notwithſtanding that I delivered thee out of moſt heinous ſins, and from eternal damnation itſelf, wherein thou hadſt juſtly lain burning many years ſince, if my mercy had not prevented thee?

5. To be ſhort, why wilt thou deſpiſe me, ſeeing I have ſo often preſerved thee from committing of many offences, and alſo

raised thee out of the bottomless gulf of sin and wickedness? What, dost thou not yet at length consider that thou art vile, miserable, and merely nothing, but by my grace? And how then darest thou lift up thy face to behold me, whom thou hast so often offended, so long time despised, in so sundry ways contemned? I speak these things, my Daughter, to the end that thou shouldst know thyself.

6. Consider how vile and filthy thou art in thy body, how much polluted in thy soul, and how impure in thy heart. And lastly, remember how unclean thou hast altogether made thyself with wicked works, with filthy cogitations, with corrupt and impure affections, and yet, nevertheless, how I still forbear to punish thee; nay, notwithstanding all this, how I declare my love towards thee, with pouring my benefits daily upon thee; but how long must I do this? Till what time must I forbear with thee? When wilt thou come to know thyself? How long wilt thou stay to return unto me? Why dost thou not humble thyself under my yoke? Dost thou not see that I am

not longer able to withhold my mercies from thee? Doft thou not perceive how I have called thee; in what place I have planted thee? Where are thy fruits? Doft thou not know how I wink at all thine iniquities, all thine abominations, all thine unthankfulnefs?

7. Yet I fpeak not thefe things, O my Daughter, to upbraid thee with thofe benefits which I have heaped upon thee, but, as it were, languifhing with love of thee; and as it were, feeming to ftand in need of thee (though indeed I ftand in need of nothing); yea, being, as it were, not able to live without thee, I do invite thee to love me again for that unfpeakable goodnefs and charity which I have fhewed towards thee, that by loving me thou mayeft perfectly fee what I am, and what thou art; how much I have done for thee, and how injurious, on the contrary, thou haft fhewed thyfelf unto me for the fame.

8. Moreover, confider how many and innumerable fouls are in hell at this day, and how thou haft been far more wicked than they, and more juftly deferved that

place, if thou hadſt not been withholden from it by my grace. Imagine likewiſe, that if they had received as much grace from me as thou haſt done, they would have ſhewed themſelves much more thankful unto me than thou haſt been. If thou conſidereſt all theſe things, that is, my Majeſty, and thine own baſeneſs, how proud thou art in thy baſeneſs, and how humble I was in my Majeſty; how far for thy ſake I abaſed myſelf to all poverty and contempt, it would not ſeem ſo great a matter to thee to humble thyſelf.

9. If, I ſay, thou wouldſt rightly ponder with thyſelf, in how much poverty, in how abject eſtate, and in how great contempt, I, being ſo mighty, ſo rich, of ſo high dignity—that is, exceeding all meaſure in majeſty, and infinite in goodneſs, and incomprehenſible in them both—was content to ſerve thee, ſo baſe, and ſo vile a creature, ſcarce worthy the name of man—yea, and did it with ſo great charity, fidelity and deſire—there would, by the impreſſion of theſe thoughts, be bred in thy heart ſo great an obedience towards me, ſo great a

reverence of me, and fo great a defire to ferve and adore my Majefty, as can neither be expreffed in words nor conceived in thought. It would procure, moreover, in thee an infatiable defire and moft burning thirft to honour me, to worfhip me, to exalt me, and to contemn, humble and defpife thyfelf, and for the love of me to throw thyfelf under the feet of all my creatures, and, befides, patiently to endure reproaches, contempt, and injury, at all their hands.

10. For though thou doft humble thyfelf never fo far, though thou beareft never fo much, yet thou fhouldft think that thou hadft endured nothing in refpect of the thirft and defire thou feeleft in thine own mind to abafe thyfelf, and exalt me; infomuch that thou fhouldft moft love thofe who did feek moft to opprefs and defpife thee, becaufe they did ferve in this behalf, to fatisfy thine earneft defire and thy humility, when they thought fo much to humble and abafe thee. If thou feeleft not, my Daughter, thefe things as yet in thyfelf, acknowledge how unthankful thou art, and how far from true humility, which is a

sincere and most lowly submission of thy heart in the sight of my Divine Majesty. After which followeth ever a contempt of thine own self; and a will likewise not only to be despised of others, but even by them to be acknowledged most vile.

11. I exhort thee once again, my Daughter, to look into my humility, and to take example by it, how thou shouldst humble thyself. See how the world despised my life and doctrine, how they did falsely accuse and utterly reject me, how they backbited me in all their speeches, how great reproaches, scorns, contempts, and derisions I suffered, even as a reprobate of most vile persons, and for most vile and unthankful creatures. And being thus mocked and made most abject as a scorn of all men, yet I despised no man, neither did I excuse myself, nor any way sought in speech to resist or reprove them. Recount also with thyself, O unthankful creature, which art worthy to be despised, thine own obstinacy, negligence, sins, ingratitude, inconstancy, vileness; and lastly, how thou art nothing of thyself, but by my grace only. Bewail,

lament, and excuſe thyſelf of all theſe before me with continual tears. Whatſoever ſhall happen unto thee, turn it to thine own benefit, and uſe it as a means to make thee humble. Take heed that thou takeſt not pleaſure in thyſelf, but rather wonder how thou canſt pleaſe or delight any other, if they did rightly know thee. Ever fix the eyes of thy heart upon the conſideration of thine own weakneſs, and diſability in all reſpects.

12. Conſider how thou art nothing, and what thou oughteſt to be and art not; likewiſe what thou haſt not, and how unable thou art to do any good; how many things thou wanteſt; and, to be ſhort, how far thou art from true and perfect charity, and from the perfection of a holy man's life. Call to mind alſo how unlike, and how little agreeable thou art unto me, and remember that merely thou haſt no good thing at all of thyſelf, but receiveſt all good things from me only, without any other means whatſoever. Moreover, make account that thou haſt of thyſelf theſe things, and no other at all; that is, an apt inclination to

sin, to offend, to rebel, to stand in need of all good things, to be in necessity and misery, and by thine own fault both to lose, and overthrow all those blessings and graces which I bestow upon thee. For it is most certain, that if I should leave the nature of man to her own liberty, and to do that whereunto she is most inclined, she would do no good at all, but decline every day from worse to worse, seeing she runneth so vehemently headlong now to commit wickedness; notwithstanding that I do so earnestly forbid her, and in a manner violently withhold her. For the nature of man is nothing, and hath nothing of herself, and laboureth after that which is nothing. If thou didst continually meditate upon this, it would help thee very much for procuring of humility.

13. There must be also, notwithstanding, joined unto this, another kind of humiliation, for thy hidden and unknown imperfections, which for the most part are very grievous, although thou being purblind dost not perceive them. Fall, therefore, prostrate for these before the feet of my

mercy, and bewail from thy heart thy incurable aptnefs and infirmity to commit fin, neither think ever otherwife of thyfelf than of one that is guilty of many faults, blind in many things, and moft unthankful of all creatures.

Chap. XIX.
How we Ought not to Care for Men's Judgments.

TROUBLE not thy mind with imagining what men think of thee, nor what cenfure they give of thee, neither yet fear their judgment, fo long as thou doft not wittingly (as far as lieth in thy power) give them any fcandal or occafion juftly to reprehend or backbite thee. For thou art neither the better if they commend thee, nor the worfe if they difpraife thee. But thou art in truth as I account thee, and as thou fheweft to be in my fight. Therefore, let not the commendation of any other rejoice thee, nor yet their difpraifes grieve thee. For what doſt thou gain by the commendation of others? Nothing, truly; but it doth rather many times greatly hurt thee, becauſe it deceiveth thee, and puffeth thee up with pride and vanity. And, on the contrary part, what can the contempt, reprehenſion, abaſing, backbiting, condemnation, and perſecution of men hurt thee? Truly, nothing at all; but rather they profit thee much, for they bring thee to know thyſelf, and help thee not a little to obtain humility of life and amendment of thy manners. For by it thou ſhalt be made more wary and wiſe in thy converſation with men, and not to truſt in them, but to put all thy confidence in me.

2. The judgment of men, therefore, is not much to be cared for, whether they ſpeak good or evil of thee. Let them think what they will, in the meantime lift thou up thy heart unto me, and if by ſearching every ſecret corner of thy heart, thou findeſt nothing in it that may offend me, fear nothing; but if by this examination thou findeſt ſomewhat wherein thou haſt offended me, bewail thy fault, not becauſe men do

despise thee, for thou oughtest then justly both to suffer and desire that, but because thou hast offended me, and also given other men by thine example occasion to sin. But if anything be commended or dispraised in thee which is not sin, be not otherwise, or more moved therewith, than if some other man were commended or dispraised.

3. If men praise thee, ascribe it to their error and good-will towards thee; if they reprove thee, or condemn thee, marvel not at it. For what marvel is it, if men reprove, despise, and condemn thy life, seeing they also reproved my life, and condemn all my doctrine, which was most innocent, void of all spot, and which could by no means be justly reprehended. Rejoice rather that thou art come to walk in those steps which I had trodden before, that is, if being humbled and accounted as a castaway of all men, and be glad that thou suffereth these persecutions of men. Let others imagine mischief against thee, I will turn their mischiefs to thy benefit; only endure thou all patiently, and be silent.

4. Study in all things to please me, and

not men; and yet if thou chanceſt to pleaſe men, think that they are deceived in their opinion of thee, becauſe they know thee not as well as I do, but do judge thee through their own ſimplicity, according to that appearance of goodneſs which they ſee in thy outward ſhow. But if thou doſt diſpleaſe them, impute it to thine own deſerts, and let it make thee more humble; for if they do deſpiſe thee for ſo little faults as they are able to ſee in thee, what would they do if they ſaw as perfectly as I all thy ſins and offences? Delight, therefore, to be accounted vile and contemptible, and though thou be deſpiſed never ſo much, yet think that thou deſerveſt to be a great deal more deſpiſed than thou art.

5. Thou oughteſt to account thyſelf moſt miſerable, moſt unworthy, moſt unthankful, and moſt needing of my grace and mercy, of all other creatures; remembering always, that of thyſelf thou art merely nothing, and that all thy works which are without me neither favour anything of virtue nor yet are any thing worth. Whoſoever is moſt wicked, think him better and more worthy

of heaven than thyself. Believe that other men do merit, and think that thou art tolerated here by my mercy only. Presume not, therefore, in these respects, to compare thyself with any man, but imagine that thou hast offended me more than all men, and that thou art more vile and unthankful to me than any creature that liveth; because whatsoever is of thyself, either is nothing at all, or else is sin. Wherefore, to extol or magnify thyself, by the means of those gifts which thou hast wholly received from me, is intolerable, and a point of most arrogant pride. For the preventing whereof, and for thy greater profit, I do often withdraw from thee my sensible blessings, because thou knowest not how to use them, but abusest them, in turning them only to the magnifying of thyself, whereas in truth thou oughtest to challenge or ascribe nothing to thyself, but wholly attribute all unto me.

6. Take heed, therefore, that in the petitions which thou makest unto me thou hast no respect to thyself, but to me only, lest thou shew thyself unthankful towards me

by pride, or deteſtable in my ſight by thine own negligence. Remember how thou art nothing of thyſelf, how quickly thou art vanquiſhed when I do not protect thee; and conſider how thou art not able to endure the ſmalleſt adverſity, or overcome the weakeſt temptation, when I fight not for thee. For of thine own ability thou haſt no other power in the world, but only to corrupt and pollute what good thing ſoever I beſtow upon thee.

7. Thou art too apt, my Daughter, to diſpraiſe other men, which is a token, without doubt, of great arrogancy, as though thou wert worthy to be preferred before thoſe which thou ſo diſcommendeſt, becauſe thou perhaps wanteſt that vice whereof thou accuſeſt them, and yet are ſubject to many others. If thou wert not blind, thou mighteſt perceive that thou deserveſt not by this kind of dealing, in any ſort to be preferred before them; but rather thine own tongue maketh thee more deteſtable than they, becauſe it diſcovereth openly thine arrogancy or envy. My friends are wont to reproach and accuſe themſelves of their

own vices, and not to find fault with others; for they fufpect both their works and themfelves, neither will they truft themfelves in any thing, becaufe they have been by that means fo often deceived. For they fear always that they feek not me with fuch fincerity as they ought. Befides, they wonder at and commend other men's works, for they will not be brought to fufpect any evil of their neighbours. Therefore, do thou always either praife or excufe others, or elfe fay nothing at all, having ever before thine eyes only thine own vilenefs and unthankfulnefs, and wondering that all men do not reprove and deteft thee.

8. Thou canft not, my Daughter, obtain humility, except thou love to be humbled, for it is of neceffity that a mind difpofed to be humbled muft ever go before humility. Receive, therefore, all things which I fend unto thee, as means to humble thee. Delight alfo to be humbled and contemned of others; fuffer thy good name to be flandered; hold thou thy peace, and refer thy caufe unto me; I know better than thou doft how to defend thy good name. But

if thou fighteſt for thyſelf, thou needeſt not my protection. If thou doſt with humility and patience bear all, and be ſilent, I will chooſe a time wherein I will anſwer for thee. Do not thou, by defending of thyſelf, prevent my gracious determination towards thee. I will fight for thee, and will have thee to be patient and ſilent.

Chap. XX.

Of Obedience.

OBEDIENCE is a moſt excellent virtue, and moſt acceptable unto me; that work which in itſelf is vileſt, and leaſt of all others, if it be done merely for obedience only, it is better accepted of me, and more profitable and meritorious unto him that doth it, than infinite others which men do voluntary, and to pleaſe their own appetite. Neither canſt thou offer unto me, believe me, my Daughter, a more noble and worthy ſacrifice, than to preſent me with a humble heart, obedient and ready to do all things that I shall command. For it may so fall out, as a man by obedience only may clean leave and forsake himself for my sake, and so profit more by denying of his own will, and be more inwardly united unto me, than if he had bestowed much time in other most noble exercises.

2. Wherefore thou oughtest, my Daughter, to be always as obedient unto me as if I were ever present with thee in a corporal form, and that thou didst as continually enjoy my presence as a wife doth her husband, with whom she dwelleth. When any man shall call thee from me, to do some act of obedience, thou oughtest to leave me and obey him. For this is not a forsaking of me, but a forsaking of thyself; because thou preferrest my honour and my will before thine own convenience and consolation, in that thou dost according to my commandments deny thyself, and seekest not thine own convenience, but the benefit of others. In this sort shouldst thou relinquish thyself, and all care to please thyself, or to seek thine own convenience. For so shouldst thou not leave me, but find that

which is a hundred times more worthy and profitable for thee than thofe things which thou forfakeft.

3. Learn therefore to leave thyfelf for my fake, that is, by denying of thine own will, to want that fruit, that confolation, and that profit which thou defireft to reap; for by doing thy duty in this fort, both thou honoureft me, and not only lofeft nothing in thy profit, but alfo obtaineft things, although it be by another means, that are a hundred times better. Wherefore efteem nothing fo precious, neither account thou anything fo profitable, as that thou wilt not be drawn from it willingly, for obedience' fake, with a mind wholly refigned to my pleafure. For whatfoever the thing be, that for the love of it, either thou refufeft to perform thine obedience, or comeft to do it grudgingly or unwillingly, it is the idol of thine own appetite: more pernicious to thee than can be expreffed. If thou be in a place where thou haft no fuperior, or where thyfelf is fuperior, make all men thy fuperiors, obeying their will, and forfaking thine own. Marry, do it not of flothfulnefs,

but wheresoever thou mayest even of thine own desire and of purpose to renounce thyself for my sake.

4. Love the virtue of obedience from the bottom of thy heart, and leave it not as long as thou livest, not only to thy superiors, but also yield, obey, and subject thyself, (whensoever thou art not restrained by my will) in all things, and to all men for my sake, and that without being grieved with it, repining at it, or disputing about it. And because thou mayest do this the more frankly, respect not the man who by my ordinance is thy superior, whether he be learned or meet for the office; neither seek to mark or consider whether he be learned or unlearned, an excellent man or a base person. But have regard to this only, that he is by my providence made thy superior, by whom I will govern thee, and in whom thou oughtest to hear me, ask counsel of me, and obey me.

5. Therefore resist not, but yield to this my providence, seeing if I appoint such a man, I have as much care to rule thee, and to make thee subject unto me by the means of so simple a person, as by him that is

learned. Yea, I have the like regard of thy well-doing, by any whomsoever it shall be my pleasure to appoint over thee. Wherefore I would have thee subject thyself unto him, without any servile fear, or scruple of thy conscience, and despising thine own counsel and wisdom, submit thyself to be governed by his judgment and opinion. Whatsoever he shall determine or appoint thee, accept it from his mouth as from mine own. For I place such superiors over my servants sometimes, as have small learning, and are little practised in those exercises, to the end that they should not regard man's wisdom, or respect in the man himself; but rather me in the man, that am their God, and as well able to answer them by a simple man (if they can have faith and confidence in me) as by a learned.

6. And therefore, whatsoever they shall be answered, or howsoever they shall be counselled at his hand, let them receive it, not as from a man, but as from myself, attributing all to me and my direction, and ascribing nothing to the man, whether he be wise or simple. If thou wouldst not,

therefore, go aftray, walk in the path of obedience, and do nothing at all without the counfel of thy Paftor, or Ghoftly Father, or fuperior. Live always in fimplicity and poverty of fpirit, renouncing quite thine own judgment, thine own counfel, thine own fenfe, and thine own opinion; neither take any occafion at any time to complain or murmur, efteeming that always beft which thy fuperior, or (if thou haft none) what other fhall think fitteft, as long as it is not manifeft and apparent fin. And, therefore, fully to mortify and kill in thyfelf thine own will, thou fhouldft not only be obedient unto men, but alfo fubject thyfelf unto all my creatures for my fake.

7. For thou oughteft fo much to hate thine own will, and thou fhouldft fo much defire to extinguifh it, that thou fhouldft live amongft men, wherefoever thou art, even as if thou wert clean without any will of thine own; that is, as if thou madeft no election or choice of any one thing more than another, but accepted of all things indifferently that chanced unto thee, excepting this only, that another man's will

(if thou knowest it) must ever please thee better than thine own, so that it be without sin, and that honesty and discretion be observed in it. Yield, therefore, unto all men in those things which are thine; that is, in those things which do properly and only belong unto thyself, in such sort, as if thou hadst professed obedience to them all. Nay, whensoever thou shalt be alone, do not thine own will, but dispose of thyself so as thy whole course of life, and all thy exercises, may tend to the renouncing of thyself. For this shall be better and more profitable unto thee than the joys of Paradise.

8. And whensoever that my will shall be made known unto thee, whether it be by inward inspiration, or by the Scripture, or by thy superior, or by some other creature of mine, or by any other means; whensoever, also, that thou shalt be inwardly admonished by me, straight despise all that thou hast of thyself, as thine own counsel, thine own judgment, thine own appetite, thine own opinion, thine own liking, or thine own inclination, and follow my will. But thou must have a special

care wifely to learn what my will is, left thou mayeft think that thou art governed by my fpirit, when in truth thou art directed by thine own, or elfe by the fpirit of error or deceit. To avoid this, therefore, do all things according to the counfel of thy fuperior, and fubmit thyfelf wholly to his will and direction.

Chap. XXI.
How we muft Mortify our own Will and Defire.

NOTHING can do thee mifchief, O Daughter, but thine own will, which, if thou haft once mortified, no other creature can hurt thee; for what creature can hurt thee if thou art dead to thyfelf, and haft mortified thine own defire? That is, if thefe words, or rather the affection of thefe words, be mortified in thee, to wit, I, and me, and to me, and mine, which is as much as to fay, as if there be no refpect in the world in thee, to pleafe thyfelf, or to ferve thine own appetite; who could hurt thee when I live in thee, and thou in me, whom no creature can resist, but is enforced to serve? Marry, if thou wilt follow or retain still within thee thine own will, all things will resist thee, all things will fight against thee, and in despite of thy teeth, whether thou wilt or no, thou must yield in the end, and canst no way escape my providence, although it will be then as a cross to torment thee, and not as a consolation to rejoice thee.

2. But if thou renouncest quite thine own will, thou shalt taste an inward peace and joy, which that sensual appetite of thine neither knoweth nor is able to conceive; for nothing troubleth the world, but everybody seeking to please their own appetite. Therefore I said to my disciples:—In the world, that is, in those things which are of the world, to wit, your own desires, which the world seeketh to satisfy, you shall have distress; but have confidence, for I have overcome the world, that both you may overcome in me, and have peace in me also. Begin, therefore, thou also, and taking out this lesson, both mortify and pluck up by the very roots all the desires of the

world and all felf-love out of thy heart. Otherwife, how canft thou overcome the world or the devil, if they have their army within thee?—that is, if they have vices lodged within thy foul? Throw out quickly whatfoever is in thee contrary to my will, and whatfoever fighteth againft thee in thy fpiritual warfare. For neither the world nor the devil can ever come to vanquifh thee, or in a manner to refift thee, but by the help of thofe things which they poffefs in thee.

3. Wherefore they which do perfecute thy vices, which do opprefs thee, which fhew unto thee, and lay before thine eyes, thine own weaknefs; to be fhort, which offend thee, that is, which offend thine own will in thee, and confequently thyfelf, becaufe thine own will and felf-love reigneth in thee. (For otherwife they could not offend thee, for that thefe things, to wit, thy felf-will and thy felf-love, are only hurt and offended); they, therefore, as I faid, which do thus offend thine own will in thee, which fhew thee how thou haft not mortified thine own appetite, are thy fpecial friends and benefactors. Thefe thou

oughteſt to love, and withal to be glad, becauſe they do perſecute thine own appetite, which is thy worſt adverſary, and only dangerous enemy. Therefore, if thou wilt wiſely uſe and take the benefit of this occaſion, the more that thine own will is repreſſed in thee, the ſtronger thou ſhalt grow, and the greater force thou ſhalt have.

4. The leſs rule that thine own appetite hath over thee, the more intereſt have I ſtill in thee, and the further that it is baniſhed from thee, the more fully do I poſſeſs thee; becauſe following of thine own will, if it do thee no other hurt, yet it doth ever certainly bring this miſchief upon thee, that it ſuffereth not me to have operation and poſſeſſion in thee. Wherefore it depriveth thee of me, which am infinite goodneſs itſelf. For though thou labour never ſo much, and deviſe never ſo many means, thou ſhalt never find any other way to come unto me than this, which I have taught my diſciples, ſaying:—He that will come after me, let him deny himſelf, that is, let him leave, mortify, and quite forſake his own will, take up his croſs and follow

me. Begin, therefore, with this, for this of neceffity thou muft do; whatfoever thou forfakeft, if thou forfakeft not thyfelf, thou haft forfaken nothing. And contrariwife, if thou poffeffeft not thyfelf, but leaveft thyfelf to be poffeffed by me, thou haft forfaken all things for my fake, although thou liveft in all abundance of wealth and honour. The more that thou goeft out of thyfelf, the farther do I enter into thee, and as much as thou doft die unto thyfelf, fo much do I live in thee. If thou difpleafeft thyfelf, I will be the fweeter unto thee.

5. Forfake, therefore, all things, that thou mayeft find all things; that is, forfake thyfelf, that thou mayeft find me. How long wilt thou ftay, my Daughter? How long wilt thou ftand ftill amazed? All thy diftrefs proceedeth only of that extreme felf-love which poffeffeth thy heart, and of the fmall confidence which thou haft in me. Forfake, therefore, thyfelf, and believe me. Doft thou think that I can deceive thee? Why doft thou not commit thyfelf to me? Why doft thou not truft in my goodnefs? What art thou able to profit thyfelf,

or what good canſt thou do to thyſelf?
What art thou without me? Art thou in
any danger if, committing thyſelf to me,
thou renounceſt thine own will? See to
whom thou commit thyſelf! To me, verily,
without whom thou ſhouldſt have no being
at all, or be anyways able to ſtand, much
leſs than to be ſafe or well. Wilt thou,
then, commit thyſelf unto me, with whom
thou canſt never be ill? Wilt thou, then,
commit thyſelf unto me, who cannot reject
thee, who cannot forſake thee, who cannot
deceive thee, who cannot but love thee?
Throw thyſelf into my arms, I pray thee,
and rely thyſelf wholly upon me, with confidence, and without delay I will receive
thee, I will preſerve thee. Without me
thou art as though thou wert not at all;
therefore if thou loveſt thyſelf, reject thyſelf and embrace me, that I may alſo embrace thee, and unite thee ſo cloſe unto me,
as no man ſhall be able to hurt or touch
thee, but that he muſt firſt of neceſſity hurt
and touch me.

6. Wherefore, leave thyſelf with a glad
and willing mind, that thou mayeſt neither

seek, wish, or choose this or that, of any respect, love, or inclination, which thou carriest to thyself, but let all things be indifferent to thee, only thou shouldst for my sake esteem that dearest, and desire that most, which thou knowest is most acceptable unto me. For thou oughtest to meditate of that prayer always in thy heart, which I offered unto my Father in the garden, when I was going to my passion, saying:—O Lord, thy will be done. Likewise,—Not mine, but thy will be done. And this also,—Teach me to do thy will, because thou art my God. Or else this,—Let it be done unto me according to thy good pleasure.

7. But wilt thou know how much thou hast forsaken thyself, or how much thou hast mortified thine own will? See, when loss of anything, when reproaches, when injuries do happen unto thee, whether thou art troubled with them, and whether thou art more troubled when they happen to thee than when they happen to other men. By this thou shalt find the love which thou bearest to creatures; yea, thou

shalt perceive the affection which thou carriest to thyself. For thou dost, therefore, love temporal goods; thou dost, therefore, love honour; thou dost, therefore, love quiet; and thou dost, therefore, love such miserable and transitory things, because thou lovest thyself. For thou wishest to enjoy these things, whereas, if thou didst love me, thou shouldst rather banish all these things quite from thy heart for my sake, and take all adversity as willingly as thou wouldst possess happiness. To be short, thou shouldst not be more, but rather much less, troubled when adversity happeneth to thyself than when it happeneth to others. For thou shouldst never be grieved with any accident in this world, but only when thou shewest thyself irreverent or contemptuous towards me.

8. Therefore, he that will forsake himself, my Daughter, his only labour, exercise, and the whole scope of his desire, must tend not partly, but altogether, to mortify his own appetite, to renounce his own will, to be transformed into a new shape, and to be in all sort free, and delivered from any

impediment whatſoever which lyeth in the way, and maketh a diviſion betwixt him and me. The leaſt impediments are cogitations and forms of creatures which men frame in their mind ; the greateſt is a man's own will, which the ſtronger it is, and the larger place that it occupieth and poſſeſſeth in a man, the leſs I am preſent there, and ſo conſequently the leſs do I poſſeſs in his ſoul. As long, therefore, as thou findeſt an inclination or natural deſire to one thing more than another, thou art not yet perfectly mortified, but thou haſt ſomewhat remaining in thee, which thou muſt mortify and extinguiſh.

9. What motion ſoever thou feeleſt in thyſelf, that proceedeth not from me ; what thing ſoever goeth about to buſy, alter, or poſſeſs thy mind ; what likeneſs ſoever of anything doth labour to imprint itſelf within thy heart ; whatſoever ſeeketh to draw thy liking to it, or to grieve or overwhelm thee ; endeavour thou with a recollected mind, cloſe ſhut within itſelf, and lifted up to me, lightly to paſs over, and careleſsly to deſpiſe all hope and fear,

gain and loſs, quiet and labour, joy and grief, mirth and ſadneſs, and all ſuch things as may ſeek to poſſeſs thy heart with all affection that thou mayeſt carry towards them. For if thou fix thy mind upon me, thou ſhalt eaſily tread all theſe things under thy feet. But if thou loveſt thyſelf, if thou haſt not wholly renounced thine own ſelf, thou ſhalt always feel, by following of thine own appetite, joy and grief, anger and fear, care, and infinite other paſſions.

10. Wherefore thou canſt never be quiet, except thou haſt clean mortified thyſelf, and forgotten thine own ſelf wholly. Thou muſt quite abandon thyſelf, that thou mayeſt live in me only, and bend thyſelf to be wiſe in me only, and be ſenſible to feel nothing but me only. Thou ſhalt want nothing, if thou be content in this ſort to want thyſelf. Thou ſhalt want nothing as long as thou art with me; I will have care of thee, I will protect thee; thou canſt loſe nothing in loſing of thyſelf after this ſort, for thou ſhalt find in me that which is a hundred times better than

the things which thou haſt loſt for my ſake.

11. Caſt, therefore, all thy care, all thy trouble, all thy fear, and even thyſelf alſo upon me, and commit thyſelf to me. Hope and truſt in me; thy hope cannot deceive thee, neither can it poſſibly be too great, if thou leadeſt a good and penitent life. Whatſoever thou wouldſt complain of to a man that is thy friend, reveal the ſame unto me. I will take care of thee, I will maintain thee, I will defend thee. Wherefore ſee that thou regard me only, being quite baniſhed from thyſelf within thee; that thou mayeſt mortify and extinguiſh thyſelf, that is, by rooting out thy deſires, thy ſelf-love, thy ſenſual appetites, and by renouncing all thoſe delights of thine, which thou didſt deſire before, and for which unlawful deſires I was not thy GOD, nor thou my ſervant. O, my Daughter, thou oughteſt to labour with all thy force, that thou mayeſt attain to this obedience, this forſaking of thine own will for my ſake, and thou oughteſt to reſign thyſelf ſo wholly unto me, and ſo far to ſubject

thyself to my will, as thou shouldst have no other will at all in thyself, but only that which is my will and pleasure.

Chap. XXII.

Of the Confideration of God's Providence.

AS long as there remaineth any choice, election, or inclination in thee, that moveth thee to take more pleasure, to be better contented, and to receive greater confolation by one thing than by another, there resteth something of thine own in thee, and thou hast not yet fully renounced thyself. For thou oughtest to take all things indifferently and equally, without either more joy or more grief at one time than another, and only to depend and rely upon my providence. For this course would procure thee the greatest liberty, the greatest peace, and the greatest quietness to thy soul.

2. Stand not, therefore, upon thyself, believe not thine own wit or thine own force, trust not in thine own ability, promise

thyself nothing upon thine own warrant, build nothing upon thine own imagination, and do nothing of thine own head; neither have confidence in thine own profiting, or in thine own will, although it be indeed good. But forsaking in all sorts thine own self, go out of thyself, and renouncing quite all the property which thou hast in thyself, rest and repose thyself in me only, trust in my goodness, rely upon my grace, and upon my providence. Be ready at all times without any choice, without any difference and without any murmuring in thy heart, to receive for the fulfilling of my pleasure, adversity as willingly as prosperity, both temporally and eternally, desiring always this only thing, that thou mayest ever be in all respects according to my will.

3. And, therefore, regard not how much or how little thou profitest, how near or how far thou art from me, how great or how small gifts thou hast of me; nor yet, whether thou shalt be in Purgatory or no, how long or when thou shalt suffer those pains, but refer thyself wholly to my pro-

vidence, and defire nothing but that thou mayeft ever be found beft contented with that which agreeth moft with my pleafure, and wifh not for any greater good, neither think that greater can poffibly happen unto thee, than that my firft, laft, and moft laudable will be fulfilled in thee. Wherefore feek to pleafe me in all fuch fort as is moft agreeable to my will; let my will be both thy perfection and the meafure of thy perfection.

4. Trouble not thy heart with any queftion or imagination of future things; take no care for thofe things that are uncertain, and may happen, but leave all thefe things to me, who governeth all, for it may fo fall out, as that evil which is expected or feared may not happen; or if it do happen, when it is prefent, fufficient for the day is the evil thereof. For howfoever, and whatfoever doth by my permiffion chance unto thee, my providence ought to pleafe thee above all things, and thou oughteft to praife me for it, and to hold this as an undoubted truth, that that is ever beft for thee which doth fo happen

unto thee, and that it was forefeen and appointed by my gracious hand, to fall upon thee for thy commodity; as thou doſt with a full confidence wholly depend upon my goodneſs. To conceive well of me, to truſt firmly in me, to commit themſelves altogether unto me, theſe things, I ſay, are, as it were, trumpets, whereby men do found out my goodneſs. And, therefore, when I find theſe things in any man, they pleaſe me ſo much, as I can never forſake him, nor ſuffer any evil or dangerous thing to happen unto him, who hath thus ſettled his hope in me.

5. The greater hope and truſt, therefore, that thou haſt in me, the more fully and perfectly thou ſhalt obtain thy deſire. And whatſoever ſhall happen unto thee, if thou believeſt that I am ſo good and gracious as I will turn all thy adverſities, and all things that perſecute thee, or are thine enemies, to thy good, that is, to thy benefit, I will not deceive thee, but do it indeed. And if, at the leaſt, thou canſt but frame thyſelf to accept all things in this ſort, it ſhall ſo come to paſs out of all doubt,

as I have faid. Yet my devout friends are wont to pray that I may deliver them from Purgatory, and it is no ill petition.

6. But when thou art come to perfection, and prayeſt, lying proſtrate at the feet of my Majeſty, thou ſhalt defire to fatisfy my juſtice with that fmall ability which reſteth in thee, and ſhalt offer thyſelf for my glory unto Purgatory, and to fuffer for the fulfilling of my will, whatſoever it ſhall be my will to lay upon thee, and the fulfilling of my will ſhall pleafe thee more than the efcaping of Purgatory. Therefore, if thou ſhalt overcome by my grace that inordinate love and zeal which thou carrieſt toward thyſelf, and for thyſelf, to pleafe thy fenſes and thine own will, and perfectly with a full confidence wouldſt commit thyſelf unto me, and rely upon me only, thou ſhouldſt find that my grace would work wonders in thee. Study, therefore, to pleafe me, my Daughter, and with thinking of me clean forget thyſelf, and I will fo continually think of thee, and be always fuch an affiſtant unto thee as I will never forfake thee.

7. Once again I ſay unto thee, accept all things which happen unto thee, as ſent purely, ſimply, and immediately from my hand, and not from any creature, admiring, praiſing, and accepting in all things of my providence, with joy and gladneſs, and with love and thankſgiving to me for my goodneſs. For in all thoſe things which happen unto thee, I do intend and work thy ſalvation; and with a ſingular affection, being mindful of thee, I ſend and appoint theſe things for thee, to the end that thou mayeſt either do or ſuffer ſuch things as may move me to have mercy upon thee.

8. Endeavour thou, therefore, to draw out of all things which thou ſeeſt and feeleſt, and out of all things which do happen unto thee, an occaſion to praiſe and honour me, that thou mayeſt be worthy to underſtand the true cauſe why I permitted them, that is, with how great charity I ſent them unto thee, and how thou oughteſt to refer all theſe things unto my pleaſure, to truſt in me, and withal to offer thyſelf for my glory, even unto the fountain from whence they flowed, that is, unto my good-

nefs. If thou wert perfectly acquainted with this exercife, whereby thou fhouldft as willingly accept forrow as comfort at my hand, and fhouldft alfo know how to find me in every one of my creatures, nothing could then feem fo contrary and overthwart unto thee, that thou wouldft not contemn and defpife; yea, nothing could be fo contrary unto my nature and Majefty, but that it would put thee in mind to offer facrifice unto me, for I am in every creature, and without me no creature can have any being.

9. Wherefore no creature is fo near to himfelf as I, who am moft near, and inward with them all. Wherefore thou oughteft to be fo poor in fpirit, as there fhould be nothing that thou didft either love or miflike, feek or fly, fear or defire, for any refpect to thyfelf; but only for the fulfilling of my will, which at all times, and in all places, thou fhalt come wonderfully to underftand, by thofe things which I ordain and permit, if thou feekeft me with a pure mind, and haft regard to confider of my providence.

Chap. XXIII.
How we muſt bear Adverſity.

RECEIVE all adverſity and tribulation as a meſſenger and token of my grace, which approacheth towards thee. And, therefore, whenſoever thou findeſt thyſelf oppreſſed with any trouble or adverſity, rejoice, knowing that thou haſt deſerved it, and impute not that which thou ſuffereſt to anybody, but to thine own ſins; and withal give me thanks that, looking upon thee with the eyes of my mercy, I have vouchſafed to beſtow ſo much favour on thee, as to viſit, prove, and correct thee here with a rod like my child, and have not utterly rejected thee, as thou didſt deſerve. For as long as I chaſten thee, as long as I ſcourge thee, it is a ſign that I deſire thou ſhouldſt amend. But if I withdraw my correction, leaving thee wholly to thyſelf, thou ſhalt ſeem then to have reſt and be quiet, but thou art moſt unhappy, when I have withdrawn from thee that care and regard which I had of thee, and that thou art no longer in my cuſtody.

2. Whatſoever, therefore, that thou ſuffereſt, ſay unto thyſelf, I have deſerved more grievous puniſhment; but although thou hadſt deſerved none, yet thou ſhouldſt bear all thoſe adverſities which I lay upon thee, for the love of me, and for my ſake, left that otherwiſe my good pleaſure ſhould not be fulfilled, even gladly with a moſt patient and loving mind towards me, conſidering that I ſuffered ſo many grievous torments for thy ſalvation. And yet although I had ſuffered nothing, do not I deſerve that thou ſhouldſt ſuffer ſomewhat for my ſake, in reſpect of thoſe infinite benefits which I daily pour upon thee, ſeeing all that thou haſt, thou receiveſt from me only?

3. Laſtly, ſuppoſe that there were none of theſe reaſons to move thee, yet oughteſt thou to remember that thou art mine, created and made by me, and no leſs in my power, to be framed every way according to my will, than earth is when it is in the hand of the potter. And that it is,

therefore, in my power, and a part of my juftice, to do with thee whatfoever I will, and it is no more lawful for thee to gainfay me, than for the earth to gainfay the potter. For what haft thou to fay againft me, who am thy Creator, whether I fend thee comfort or forrow? But knowing that thou haft committed fo much wickednefs as thou haft done, why doft thou not rather defire that the contempt wherewith thou haft defpifed my goodnefs fhould be punifhed in thee, and thy proud and arrogant mind humbled?

4. But there is, the rather, yet another reafon to move thee hereunto ; that is, becaufe I am one which do love thee moft faithfully, and do provide all things that are beft and moft wholefome for thee. And feeing it was my will before I created thee, that thou fhouldft fuffer at this hour, and at this moment, thofe fame things which thou doft fuffer, thou oughteft to defire above all things that this, my moft loving will, being full of all fidelity and charity towards thee, may be fulfilled in thee, fo as thou fhouldft endure all thofe things which thou doft

suffer, with gladness, with a sweet kind of patience, with thanksgiving, with meekness, and with devotion in thy heart, having no wrath nor bitter thought against those who seek to lay those adversities and vexations upon thee; but rather thou shouldst take them as my ministers in this behalf, appointed and commanded by me to this purpose, and thou shouldst consider, having thine eyes fixed upon me only, with how loving, how kind, and how faithful a heart towards thee, I have sent thee these troubles for thy benefit.

5. Receive, therefore, all affliction, whatsoever falleth upon thee, as sent from my hand only, without any other means; and take it as sent by me of love towards thee for thy commodity; accept it as gladly as I do send it lovingly. And when thou suffereft no adversity, think that my goodwill is alienated from thee, and that I am offended with thee, because I withdraw afflictions and tribulations from thee, which is the noblest gift and ornament wherewith I am wont to honour and beautify my friends.

6. Recount with thyfelf how great vexations, how great perfecutions, how great contradictions, how great torments, how great and wearifome toils I fuffered; how great my moft dear Mother endured; and to be fhort, how great all my friends walking in my fteps have fuftained. Remember alfo that no man attaineth to eternal glory but by the Crofs and cup of affliction, and that there is no other way but this highway to the heavenly country, which way of neceffity thou muft pafs through, if thou defireft to enjoy our company in eternal happinefs. Laftly, confider that there is nothing fo fmall or fo little worth, which either thou doeft or fuffereft for my fake, but that thou fhalt receive a very great and glorious reward of me for it. And yet, notwithftanding, I will not have thee to ferve me, or to fuffer thefe things, in hope of reward, but only of mere love towards me. I know what reward I will give thee. I fay I will, becaufe I do not owe it thee in any other fort, than for that it is my will to beftow it upon thee. For all my gifts are of free grace.

7. Think not thou, therefore, of any reward, be not so base-minded, but think of me with a more noble, loving, and faithful heart, and submit thyself unto me, even of mere love for mine own sake, to endure whatsoever my will is to lay upon thee. If thou knowest, my Daughter, what great fruit is reaped by tribulations, thou wouldst esteem it as a great happiness to glory in crosses and afflictions. The greater adversities, therefore, that do happen unto thee, and the more contrary that they are to thy desires, yea, although they repugn such desires of thine as are to please me, the more earnestly thou shouldst endeavour patiently to suffer them, and the more wholly thou shouldst resign thyself unto me. For it is done by my will and providence, that thy will sometimes be hindered; yea, even when it is good, that by this means, for one virtue thou mayest obtain two, and withal mayest receive the reward of a good work for thy good will (although thou be not permitted to put it in execution) and for the adversity which did hinder thy will thou shalt receive a crown of patience.

8. Thou mayeſt add to all theſe, for thy further encouragement, this one reaſon alſo; that the more thy good will is tempted by adverſity, and the more faithful it is found, and the more patient it is in bearing of croſſes, and ſuch things as reſiſt it, the more glorious the crown is which I have laid up to reward it. Therefore, becauſe I love thee, I will have thee to be wholly and purely a faithful Spouſe unto me. I will have thee to ſerve me with renouncing all intereſt in thyſelf, and to go, not whither thou wilt, but whither I ſend or lead thee. Neither muſt thou ſeek withal to ſerve thine own appetite, when thou labourest in theſe things to pleaſe me; but rather as a faithful, devout, and obedient handmaid, which hath no will to do anything but that which is agreeable to the will of her miſtreſs. Thou muſt ſeek in nothing to pleaſe thyſelf, but me only, with all ſincerity and purity in thy intention, and that muſt be always moſt acceptable unto thee which I lay upon thee to ſuffer, whether it be by the hands of men, or any other means whatſoever.

9. Respect not, therefore, men; neither impute it to men, if thou sustainest any adversity. What blame doth the rod deserve if the father, seeking to correct his son, doth use it? Why then art thou angry with men, which, being my instruments, serve as a scourge to correct thee? Seek not, therefore, to resist them, or to argue against them, but have a special care that thine own impatience do not hurt thyself, and left thou lose that benefit by repining, which thou shouldst have gained by patient suffering. Be, therefore, courteous and gentle towards all men, in taking patiently whatsoever shall happen. Carry a mild countenance, and use a humble behaviour, that no anger, nor exclaiming, no dejection of thy mind, nor sorrow appear in thee, nor yet that anything may be found in thee which may make men to think that thou enduredst some affliction, or art oppressed with some trouble.

10. If any man reprove or reproach thee, shew him a mild and gentle countenance, holding thy peace, and smile with a certain kind of bashfulness and modesty, in token

of thy charity, which accepteth it in good part, and which taketh all things well, without either thinking of revenge, or remembering of an injury. Beware that thou fpeakeft not at that time above two or three words, and that with great temperance. And by this means thou fhalt fhew thyfelf fo humble and meek, as every man may prefume to reprove thee, and no man be afraid to difpleafe thee, or to ufe any reproach towards thee. Learn in all adverfity, whenfoever any man doth chide thee, reproach thee, or injure thee, to ufe filence, to bear it patiently, and to be quiet, and thou fhalt affuredly find my grace, which thou canft never attain unto by any other means, than by being quiet, and fuffering patiently whatfoever I fhall lay upon thee, being as willing, if it ftand with my pleafure, to receive adverfity as to enjoy profperity.

11. Thou haft, my Daughter and Spoufe, my life as a perfect example of patience and meeknefs; neither did I fpeak it without great reafon, when I faid, Learn of me becaufe I am meek and humble of heart,

seeing that my life was a lively pattern of patience, humility, and meekness. For in the middle of all my pains and torments, of all the derisions and blasphemies, which mine enemies used towards me, of all their cruel threatenings, of their most wicked and despiteful countenances against me, what complaint or show of repining at this dealing of theirs proceeded from me? Which of my enemies did I curse? To which of them did I speak sharply? Which of them did I answer? To which of them did I wish any harm? Nay, rather, was I not sorry for them, when I did pray for them all? Follow thou, therefore, my example, and have patience still joined with quietness and tranquillity of thy soul, and be meek without murmuring or complaining. Fight not for thyself; answer not for thyself; depend not, neither yet excuse thou thyself; hold thou thy peace, and commit both thyself and thy cause to my protection; I will fight for thee.

12. Cleave, therefore, in the meantime wholly unto me, in all quietness, without any perturbation or motion in thy soul,

being ready, with all gladnefs, rather to fuffer any confufion for my fake than either inwardly in thy mind, or outwardly in thy fhow, to ufe the leaft murmuring in the world againft me. As long as thou thinkeft that thou art wronged; as long as thou believeft, my Daughter, that thou suffereft unjuftly, or haft not deferved thofe things which thou fuffereft, thou art neither come to true patience, nor yet to a perfect knowledge of thyfelf.

13. Wherefore, I would wifh thee to be always ready with a joyful and devout heart to run and meet any adverfity that fhall light upon thee; and offer thyfelf unto me, as one that is willing to fuffer tribulations, to want all things that thou defireft, and both to take and travail, and to bear any mifery in what fort foever it fhall be my pleafure to appoint. Think that day loft wherein thou haft not received fome notable crofs. If thou kneweft what great commodity is reaped by patience, thou wouldft do great honour, and fhew great thankfulnefs to thofe that afflict thee. Confider how I, as an innocent Lamb, did

carry a moſt meek and quiet mind, void of all bitterneſs towards thoſe which did ſpit upon me, ſcourge me, and crucify me, and how I excuſed them, and prayed for them. In like ſort muſt thou do, and not count anything injury that is done unto thee; nor yet believe that injuries can be offered thee, but regard me only, reſpect me wholly, and thou ſhalt come to learn that I, and no other, have done all theſe things merely of love towards thee.

14. By doing thus, my Daughter, there is nothing in any creature which will not be a means and an occaſion for thee to obtain my grace more abundantly, becauſe thou ſhalt find me in every one of them; ſo that thou doſt contemplate upon the creature, not as a creature, but upon me in the creature, as thou oughteſt to do. And if thou doſt in this behalf as thou oughteſt, thou ſhalt receive me, thou ſhalt hear me, thou ſhalt feel me in every one of my creatures; for I do ſpeak unto thee in them all. Hearken, therefore, unto me and learn by everything that happeneth unto thee what I would have thee do, and

when thou knoweſt my will, be ever moſt ready to perform it. If thou didſt give care unto me after this manner, the world, and all things contained therein, ſhould be a book of inſtructions for thee to direct thee in that courſe which agreeth moſt with my pleaſure.

Chap. XXIV.
Of Wanting of Conſolation.

THE highway, and alſo that moſt excellent way, wherein all my perfect friends have walked, and wherein thou muſt alſo walk, is, to want all kind of conſolation, when thou art compaſſed in on every ſide with adverſity and diſtreſs, and to be ſo poor, as there may be nothing left to which thou mayeſt turn thyſelf for ſuccour, to which thou mayeſt fly unto for refuge, or in which thou mayeſt truſt; nor yet, that there .be any man whom thou mayeſt ſeek counſel of, or in whom thou mayeſt have confidence but in me only, that by this means thou mayeſt have no other thing to remain for thee to do, but only that all thy care and cogitations may tend to devife how thou mayeft profit and fet forth my glory, in fuftaining of thefe afflictions, both inwardly in thy mind, by having a defire to offer thyfelf unto them, and outwardly in thy behaviour, by ferving of all creatures, and fubjecting thyfelf unto them all, in fuch fort as if it were lawful for them, without committing any offence or doing thee any injury, to afflict thee, and tread thee under their feet; yea, as if they did in this no more than I charged and commanded them.

2. In doing thus, thou fhouldft be free from all complaining, from all difputing, from all grudging, and from all malice againft thy neighbour. And by this account thou fhouldft love thofe beft which did opprefs thee moft. Becaufe they did open the way unto thee, whereby thou mayeft come to renounce thyfelf, and gave thee an opportunity both to pleafe me, and fhew thyfelf thankful towards me. Moreover, thou fhouldft rejoice that they offered thee a good occafion to exercife virtue,

and to try thy love towards me; and thou wouldſt deſire this above all things, if thou didſt indeed perfectly love me.

3. There is yet another perfection greater than this, and in a higher degree, that is, to be deſtitute both of all earthly and heavenly conſolation, being loaded with temptations, diſtreſſes, vexations, doubts, fears, perplexities, and adverſities, and to be, as it were, utterly rejected from me and quite forgotten by me, and yet notwithſtanding all this, not to fly from me and go to my creatures, nor to depart from me and ſeek worldly help, nor yet to deſire that conſolations and revelations ſhould be imparted unto them. But ſtill to truſt in me, to expect patiently my pleaſure, to cleave unto me with a pure faith and perfect charity, and to be ready to continue in this ſtate as long as it ſhall be my will to permit it. Nay, which is more, to refer themſelves wholly unto me, and to offer themſelves to ſuffer both theſe, and by any other thing whatſoever, for the fulfilling of my will, and ſetting forth of my glory, and to praiſe me in all theſe

distresses, in such sort as they are able, although it be but with a dry and barren heart.

Chap. XXV.

Of Inward Peace and Meekness of Heart.

THOU hast understood sufficiently, my Spouse, how thou oughtest to be patient, and in patience meek; that is, how thou oughtest to bear all things with so indifferent, peaceable, and quiet a mind (for meekness is no other thing than perfect tranquillity in true patience), as nothing should be able to make thee sad, or to vex or trouble thee, whatsoever did happen unto thee, that proceeded not from me in my wrath and displeasure, whether it were for a time or for eternity, excepting this only, which thou must always carry for a firm resolution, that thou wilt never be excluded from my grace and charity, nor yet in thine own will be withdrawn or divided from me. For this thou must not neglect,

To the Faithful Soul.

but take care of above all things, that thou mayeſt always be united unto me in perfect charity.

2. Thou muſt alſo remember, in what place ſoever thou art, what pain or conſolation ſoever thou feeleſt (if the ſame be for the ſetting forth of my glory, and by my ſpecial pleaſure) that thou rejoice in it, becauſe by it thou obeyeſt my will, being ready in every ſort to be according as it ſhall beſt agree with my will, either comforted or afflicted. And when thou art ſettled in this reſolution, no loſs of any external thing that happeneth unto thee in this world can grieve thee. For nothing can chance that is contrary to thy liking, as long as my will is always thy will, and that thou haſt no other will in thee but that which is my pleaſure. Therefore then, as I ſaid, let my will be always fulfilled in all things. And it ſhould be the greateſt joy that thou couldſt have, when my will is performed in thee. For thou art then fully ſettled in thine inward man, in all peace and tranquillity, although thou findeſt in thine own outward man,

distress and desolation, which notwithstanding thou dost patiently take without any perturbation, because thy will is in all things agreeable to mine.

3. Be quiet in this manner, my Daughter, providing so as all fury, and all kind of repining be altogether extinguished in thee, and that thine irascible power or faculty be even so fully mortified in thee, as it be immovable, and not to be stirred by any accident. Let thy concupiscible power also be so established in virtue, as it may be wholly lifted up unto me. And let thy reasonable power, taking part of their joys, accord with them, so as thy conscience, enjoying peace and quietness within itself, thy whole soul may be in perfect tranquillity.

Chap. XXVI.
Of the Love which we should bear towards our Neighbour.

LET thy heart towards thy neighbour, my Daughter, be full of compaſſion, and a chaſte kind of love. I call that a chaſte love which defileth not the heart with concupiſcence, nor doth buſy it with too much familiarity, or too often keeping of company, nor doth ſtain it with any inordinate affection, nor doth diſquiet it with thoughts that procure diſtraction in thy ſoul, nor doth trouble it with importunity of vain deſires, nor doth occupy thy imagination with multitude of fancies, or impreſſions of divers things; but without choice of perſons, or regard of ſex, doth embrace all ſorts of men and women for my ſake, with abundance of charity, and for it only, without any other reſpect at all.

2. Therefore, being full of a devout kind of goodwill and pure charity, rejoice with

every one in all the benefits and commodities which they receive, whether it be touching their foul or body, and ever flowing with a kind of compaffion, which can never ceafe running. Lament with every one in their neceffities and tribulations, pouring out the ftreams of thy courtefy, affability, mercy, and pity to all men. And fee that thou art inflamed with a ready defire and willing mind to comfort them, to ferve them, to fuccour them, and to help them to bear the burden of their troubles, efteeming their corporal or fpiritual afflictions thine own, and carrying the unfpeakable affection of a moft tender mother towards all men whatfoever. Endeavour, therefore, to excufe every man, and to do them good by thy prayers, benefits, and all the pleafures that lieth in thy power. And upon fuch as thou canft beftow no other benefit, feek to mitigate their forrow with thy courteous behaviour, thy fweet fpeech, or any other means that thou art able.

3. Take fpecial heed that thou neither judgeft nor defpifeft any man, becaufe it both harmeth thy foul and, befides, dif-

pleaſeth me wonderfully. And therefore exclude, by all the means thou mayeſt, ſuſpicions, and ill-conceits of other men, from thee; excuſe alſo all thoſe who fall and offend. When thou ſeeſt one to ſin, ſay within thyſelf that he was permitted to fall for his greater amendment; that he had a good intention, and was deceived either by ignorance or error; that his infirmity being too ſtrongly aſſaulted with temptation, was enforced to yield. Say and ſpeak it unfeignedly from thy heart, that thou hadſt fallen much more heinouſly than he did if this temptation had aſſaulted thee. Thou oughteſt not with one and the ſelf-ſame but with other eyes to look upon thine own and thy neighbour's acts. For thou ſhouldſt judge of thine own with a ſevere eye, aggravating thine imperfections, and not eſteeming or ſeeking to leſſen thy virtues.

4. And on the contrary part, thou ſhouldſt make reckoning of thy neighbour's imperfections as very ſmall, and of his virtues as very great. Wherefore take care always neither to ſpeak nor hear ill of

others. Never reprove thy neighbour in anger, though he deferve to be blamed. For what doth it profit thee if thou cureſt him, and woundeſt thyſelf? Or what doth the medicine avail, if by it thou goeſt about to heal one wound, and in the meantime makeſt ten others? Expect thou a time wherein thou mayeſt have fit opportunity to reprove him, and then reprove him with the ſpirit of lenity and ſweetneſs, rather by entreating him, and exhorting him, than by handling him ſharply or roughly, making thy hearty prayers unto me, with ſorrowful groans, that this reproving of thine may be effectual, and work his ſalvation.

5. Take heed that thou art not the cauſe of breeding diſſenſion, diſcord, or hatred amongſt men, but let all thy ſpeech in all places tend to peace, being mindful that I ſaid: "Bleſſed are the peace-makers, for they ſhall be called the children of God." If any man offend thee, if any man perſecute thee with malice, requite his wrongs with benefits, his hard and four countenance with a ſweet and meek behaviour, his ſharp and reproachful words with mild and

gentle anfwers, and by this means thou fhalt more eafily bring him to the knowledge of his own fault.

6. Let all the labours, miferies, poverty, contempt, and forrows, which thou feeft men endure, put thee in mind of thofe labours, afflictions, contempts, pains, and many other fharp and grievous miferies, which I fuffered for thy fake, that thou mayeft by this means behold me, find me, perceive me, perfectly love me, daily fuffer with me, and continually be transformed into me, by every thing which thou feeft in every man.

CHAP. XXVII.

Of the Purity of the Heart.

ENDEAVOUR to have fuch purity in thy heart as, being withdrawn from all earthly cogitations, thou mayeft not addict thyfelf to any delight, nay, that thou mayeft feek no delight, or take delight in any thing, or content thyfelf with the defire of any delight whatfoever. Cut off alfo, not only unlawful thoughts, but all such as are idle and unprofitable, suffering none of them wittingly to enter into thee. Let thy firm resolution be to think nothing but either of me, or for my sake.

2. Receive not into thy heart, as near as thou canst, the similitude and forms of earthly things; but thrust out all such impressions and fancies, as soon as ever they begin to appear. Cast all thy cares and troubles upon me; be not disquieted with any thing whatsoever shall happen. Keep ever a watchful guard over thy heart, that no inordinate affection to man, woman, or any other creature; no sensual desire, no vicious passion, no concupiscence, no ill inclination, or wicked intention may rest in thee.

3. Never give thy consent that any separation, although it be never so little, remain between me and thee, and see that thou dost in nothing either seek or respect thyself, but me only, purely, simply, and wholly. Lift up thy heart in every place unto me, and keep it still raised from all earthly cogitations, that whatsoever thou

haſt to ſpeak, to deal in, or to think of, thou do firſt deal with me in it by prayer, and by the internal diſcourſe of thy ſpirit. Let every action and external buſineſs give thee matter and occaſion to pray, yea, let the very occupation and buſineſs of thy heart be no other thing but a continual and daily prayer.

4. See nothing, though it be never ſo far from the nature of prayer, ſo deformed or ſo contrary to all goodneſs, but draw thou preſently out of it ſome occaſion to pray unto me, and to praiſe my name. Let all things be means for thee to lift up thy heart, and to raiſe thy affection unto me. What fair thing ſoever thou ſeeſt, what pleaſant or delightful thing ſoever thou feeleſt, acknowledge it to proceed from me, and let it put thee in mind of my beauty and glory, that I only may be thy whole delight and conſolation. Let all things edify thee, and whatſoever happeneth unto thee, take opportunity by it to meditate upon ſomething that may be profitable for thy ſoul.

Chap. XXVIII.

How we ought to refer all the Good Things we receive to the Goodnefs of God.

CHALLENGE nothing to thyfelf by any of my works, or by the means of thofe gifts which I beftow upon thee. Thou oughteft to acknowledge my gifts to my honour, and to wonder at my liberality and charity beftowed upon thee, without any defert of thine own, and my moft gracious bounty. And withal thou muft ever have prefented before thine eyes thine own bafenefs, and how thou art of thyfelf merely nothing, that by this confideration thou mayeft not afcribe or challenge anything to thyfelf out of thofe gifts which I beftowed upon thee, neither yet be rejoiced or delighted with any thing that thou receiveft from me, or for that I have wrought any good thing in thee.

2. Thou oughteft not, I fay, for any of thefe, to rejoice in thyfelf, or be glad for thine own fake, that is, becaufe thou haft

attained to fome goodnefs, for that fhould be a rejoicing altogether in thyfelf. But thou fhouldft rejoice in me, and for my gracious bounty that I have been fo good, fo liberal, fo gentle, and fo merciful to a moft unworthy and unthankful creature. Which goodnefs of mine, the viler that thou art, doth the more manifeftly appear in thee.

3. Rejoice, therefore, in my gifts, not attributing any praife thereby to thyfelf, but afcribing the whole glory unto me. And behave thyfelf fo difcreetly in receiving any of my gifts (excepting thankfulnefs and humility, which muft ever increafe in thee) as if nothing had been given thee, nothing had been wrought in thee, and that thou didft feel no good at all; directing thine eyes to thine own unworthinefs, which art of thyfelf merely nothing; and to thine own difability, which art able to do nothing; and to thine own imperfection, which cannot attain to the fmalleft goodnefs without my grace; that by this means thou mayeft not be extolled in thine own conceit, or rejoice in thine own ability, or

flatter thyself with thine own power, but attribute all unto me only.

4. If thou feelest, therefore, any sweet inspiration, or any lightening of my grace within thee, or that by my mercy thou art enabled to do another man a benefit or good turn, thou mayest rejoice in the good which I did by thee as my instrument, but in no sort to rejoice in thyself: that is, not to flatter or please thine own appetite (for in it lyeth hidden self-love), nor to think that it was done by thine own power, but rather turn away thy heart from that which was done, and from thyself also, that thou mayest never join together these two cogitations, which is thyself and my benefit, except it be (as I said) when thou comparest my infinite goodness with thy unspeakable baseness. Suffer it to pass over for that time, as though it had not been done at all, and as though thou understood no such matter: and fix all thy cogitations in the mean season upon me, and not upon the gift which thou hast received from me.

5. Look never, therefore, into the gift itself, neither settle thy mind in that con-

fideration, nor rejoice in it, nor yet be contented to reſt there ; neither ſtay, if thou feeleſt any motion in examining and ſearching curiouſly within thyſelf, what thou feeleſt, or what thou doeſt, or whether the motion proceed from me, or from ſome other cauſe (for this doth ever make a diviſion between thee and me, and doth ſtay thee longer from coming unto me), but rather paſs quickly through all theſe cogitations, and remove them clean from thee, and endeavour to unite thyſelf more nearly and firmly unto me. Chooſe rather not to know the things which after this ſort do buſy the mind, than with a curious ſearch to hinder my grace, and to procure thereby danger to thyſelf, either of being puffed up with pride, or of pleaſing thyſelf, or of rejoicing by the provocation of ſelf-love in thine own ability, or for thine own glory. But refer theſe, as all other things, unto me, only hold this with a reſolute and aſſured mind, for an infallible principle, that if I do grant thee any good gift, it is given merely without deſert, to an unthankful and an unworthy creature.

6. This kind of humility doth wonderfully pleaſe me, that thou ſhouldſt be afraid and troubled in reſpect of thine own baſeneſs, unworthineſs and unthankfulneſs, and be timorous with the conſideration of theſe things, and feel a ſhamefacedneſs and diſquiet thereby, and rather think that thou feeleſt no good thing at all, or that the motion proceedeth not from me, than to ſtay upon the conſideration thereof and rejoice therein. Remember alſo that I forbade my Apoſtles to rejoice in thoſe miracles which they wrought, or to take any glory becauſe unclean ſpirits did ſubmit themſelves unto them and obeyed them, although they were not ignorant, but did aſſuredly know that this gift proceeded from me.

7. In like ſort, therefore, my Daughter, glory not thou in thyſelf, neither rejoice without me, for any conſolation or gift which thou receiveſt; that is, rejoice no otherwiſe in it than may tend to the magnifying of my name, neither ſtay in conſideration of the thing itſelf (for therein doth ever ſome ſelf-love lie lurking, which

doth eafily beguile thofe that be not heedful) but rejoice in me only, that is, rejoice becaufe I have fhewed my glory, and fulfilled my will in thee. Seek no glory to thyfelf by my gifts, neither covet to ufurp or challenge to thyfelf any praife thereby, neither yet afcribe any thing to thine own ability. Afcribe nothing at all, I fay, to thyfelf or thine own power, neither fuffer any other man to attribute any thing to thine own worthinefs, nor rejoice in it, as if it were thine own act, but refer all unto me, and keep thyfelf from all manner of propriety in thyfelf, from attributing any thing to thine own worthinefs, from defiring anything for thine own pleafure, or rejoicing in any thing for thine own delight. Live without following thine own counfel, thine own judgment, thine own opinion.

8. If thou defireft, my Daughter, to be my Spoufe, keep thy heart chafte and pure, free and quite alienated from any other love but mine only, and from being poffeffed by any of my creatures, that it may be left whole for me to dwell in, which am thy Creator. As often as thou findeft any

sensual or natural love in thy mind to man, woman, or any other creature whatsoever; so often remember with sorrowful groans to lift up thy soul unto me, earnestly desiring my grace and my favour only, which is a most safe refuge, a most happy haven for thee, and that not for a time, but endless and eternal.

9. Whatsoever, therefore, doth busy thy senses with any cogitations towards any of my creatures, is neither pure nor without danger to thy soul. Whensoever, also, thy natural appetite receiveth any recreation, comfort or delight (if thou seekest to attain to a perfect purity), thou must of necessity renounce that pleasure, whether it be in words or any other earthly thing. Thou must pass over all things with a free mind, in no sort subject or in bondage unto them, nor adhering to any but me only. Take this also with thee for a certain rule, that nothing maketh a man so free from the love of himself or any other creature, and so far from being entangled with any earthly cogitation, as to despise himself and all creatures, and to account of me in his

heart, as his only precious jewel, esteeming all other things (as they are indeed) as filthy dung.

10. Make a diligent search in all thy actions, studies, and desires, what moveth thee unto them, and whether thou speakest or holdest thy peace, whether thou doest somewhat, or art at rest, look narrowly into the innermost corners of thy soul, that is, into the very marrow of thy cogitations and intentions, and thou shalt often find that the very original root and seed whereof this groweth, and from whence this doth spring, which thou thinkest divine, is merely human, impure, and a lewd seeking to please thine own appetite.

11. Take heed, therefore, that no vicious thought enter into thee, nor any inordinate lust remain in thee. Oh, if thou hadst thy heart clearly delivered from the love of every creature,—Oh, if being wholly converted unto me, thou didst desire me only, I would with as great a desire run to meet thee, and enter of mine own accord with as great affection into thy heart, as if I could not live without thee, or that without being with

thee I could not enjoy perfect happiness and contentment.

12. This course I know will seem grievous unto thee at the beginning, and it cannot be without some trouble thus straitly to note and observe in all things what thou seekest, what thoughts possess thy heart, and whensoever thou findest any cogitation that is not of me, or for my sake, presently to root it out of thy mind. This, I say, will procure thee great labour and affliction of thy spirit. For thou shalt find both thyself and thine own appetite lie lurking in many things, wherein thou must of necessity forsake both, and presently mortify any desire that is unlawful and inordinate in thee. For if thou seekest to overcome thine own nature, it followeth of necessity that thou must do it by violence and forcible means. And therefore thou shalt find as many crosses as thou hast wicked or impure inclinations, which must be mortified in thee.

13. But by this means, my Daughter, thou shalt first come to know thyself, for by seeing thine own disability and weak-

nefs in that thou canft not overcome thyfelf, thou fhalt be humbled. And whereas before thou thoughteft thyfelf to be fomewhat, thou fhalt then plainly find that thou art nothing. And if thou perfifteft in this courfe with continual and inceffant labour, that which at the firft was painful thou fhalt quickly find to be very eafy. For this diligent and daily looking into thyfelf, and examining of all thy thoughts, doth work many things in thee very profitable for thy falvation. It will fhew thee thine infirmity and imperfections, it will breed in thee forrow for thofe fins which thou findeft in thyfelf, and an earneft defire to be delivered of them. It will alfo make thee very careful to beware of many offences, and to avoid many dangers, into which otherwife thou wouldft have fallen.

14. To conclude, the labour and diftrefs which thou fuftaineft, and the toil which thou takeft to be clearly rid of thefe imperfections, and the tears which thou fheddeft (becaufe thou canft not overcome thyfelf, and clean be without thofe things

which thou wouldſt altogether forſake) ſhall be a baptiſm unto thee for the purging of thy ſoul, and for expiation of thine offences. Faint not, therefore, in thy courage, for thou ſhalt overcome all things by ſettling thy whole truſt in my mercy. Have confidence in me, and thou ſhalt find that I will make theſe croſſes light for thee, and help thee myſelf to bear part of the burthen.

Chap. XXIX.

How Divine Inſpirations ought to be Obſerved, and the Grace of God not neglected.

HAVE care, my Daughter, to abound always with virtuous cuſtoms, and to ſpend thy time in good exerciſes, that thou mayeſt uſe the ſame as a means to lift up thy heart unto me, when thou feeleſt no other great or ſenſible motions of my grace within thee. But thou ſhouldſt never addict thyſelf ſo much to thy exercife, as to prefer thine own conceits before my infpirations. For whenfoever thou haft learned to know my will (whether it be by the manifeftation of the will of thy fuperior, or by my providence, by which, of doubtful events, I do fometimes fet down a certain judgment) follow that ftraightway, and forfake thine own appetite.

2. Whenfoever alfo thou findeft a fenfible and plain motion of me with thee, prefently leave thyfelf and obey me, by following of mine infpirations. For I hold not myfelf fatisfied though thou doft ferve me, feek me, and bend thyfelf, to pleafe me; but I will have thee to ferve me in fuch fort as my will is to be ferved, that is, I will have thee clean to forfake thine own will, yea, although it be in a thing which is virtuous and commendable, to follow my will in another thing which is not half fo good, but feemeth to be vile and of no value. For the fame thing in refpect of my will,—that is, becaufe it is my pleafure, my ordinance, and my appointment to have it fo,—is not only not vile, and of no value, but very good, yea, and much better alfo

than the other. Thou muſt, therefore, often omit and alter thine exerciſes in this ſort, not of negligence, not of ſloth, not of any inconſtancy of thy heart, but of a pure and mere renouncing of thyſelf, that thou mayeſt not, in any place or in anything, ſtand upon thyſelf, but rely wholly upon me, with a firm and full confidence in me.

3. Oh, if thou kneweſt what great danger and what great loſs of ſpiritual profit is incurred by not receiving of mine inſpirations when I ſend them, and how damnable it is to reſiſt my divine motions, thy heart would even conſume for grief and very fear of my juſtice. Wherefore, my Daughter, ſtand always in fear of thine own actions, and ſuſpect thyſelf ever of unthankfulneſs towards me. Be ever in doubt that it may ſo happen unto thee for thy deſerts, as it hath happened to many others, that thou mayeſt for thy pride and ingratitude be juſtly forſaken of me, and deſervedly fall from my grace. Be humble, therefore, always having no confidence in thyſelf, but in me. Pray continually for my grace, and obſerve my inſpirations with great heed,

that thou mayeſt know what I require of thee; and it is not only ſufficient for thee to know my will, but to do it whenſoever thou ſhalt come to know it, and deſpiſing all other things whatſoever, to prefer it before any delight or contentation of thine own. And whereas I warned thee that thou ſhouldſt be afraid for loſing of my grace, and for being forſaken of me by thine own negligence and ingratitude, thou muſt have a ſpecial care that this fear proceed not of deſperation or of a weak faith, but of humility, which is ever of fear, full of hope and confidence in me.

4. If thou art not able to imitate the exerciſes of other men, be not therefore diſcouraged, or dejected in thine own mind. For thou ſhouldſt not ſo much reſpect other men's exerciſes or their virtues, ſeeing that I do diſtribute my gifts to every man according to his conſtitution by nature, and that particular vocation whereunto I call him, and agreeable to that ſcope and certain end whereunto I appoint him. I furniſh him alſo with divers exerciſes, fit for him, which are unfit for many others,

and not meet for everybody, becaufe the nature or vocation of particular men, to the which my grace for the moft part is accommodated and made agreeable, is different, and many times very contrary. If, therefore, thou canft not follow other men's exercifes of virtue, yet thou mayeft imitate their virtues, for they are not different, but one and the fame in all. As for example, thou mayeft be humble, thou mayeft be merciful, thou mayeft be patient, and thou mayeft refemble other men in the very fame virtues, though thou canft not imitate them in the very fame exercifes. For there is but one way to pleafe me, which hath been to all my holy fervants ever one, uniform and the fame.

5. This is the way of charity, which hath many and fundry exercifes of my holy fervants, directed to one end, and which thou muft walk, by whatfoever means I fhall appoint unto thee. If thou walkeft in this way of charity, that is, if thou follow me, by receiving of all things as from me, by committing of all things unto me, by humbling thyfelf under my mighty hand, by

yielding thyfelf unto me, by refpecting me only, and feeking my glory in all things that either thou doft or fpeakeft, I will not fuffer thee to go aftray, though thou walkeft in never so great darknefs or ignorance, though thou art vexed with never fo great temptation or diftrefs, and though thou thinkeft thyfelf never· fo quite forfaken or rejected by me.

6. Have thou, therefore, confideration always of thy vocation or calling, and ufe exercifes agreeable to the fame, being ever ready to leave them, change them, difcontinue them, and refume them, according as thou fhalt be directed by my infpiration, providence, and good pleafure. For thou fhouldft not meafure thy perfections by this or that man's account, nor by thine own eftimation. But thou oughteft to meafure it by my good pleafure, refigning thyfelf wholly thereunto, that thou mayeft not feek to attain to this or that man's perfection, or to fuch as thou defireft thyfelf, but to fuch as my will is to appoint thee.

7. Let that perfection, therefore, which

thou defireſt confiſt either in abundance or fcarcity, according to my will and good pleafure. Wiſh and pray that thou mayeſt be fuch an one in my fight, as my fpecial will is to have thee. Obferve diligently, and learn both to know and follow the infpiration of my grace. If thou neither feekeſt to pleafe thyfelf in thy natural inclinations, nor in thy fpiritual exercifes, but refpeɛt me only with a pure intention, thou ſhalt quickly find the way wherein I would have thee to walk, and the courfe which my defire is thou ſhouldſt always hold.

Chap. XXX.

How we muſt employ the Gifts of God which we receive to the Benefit of Others.

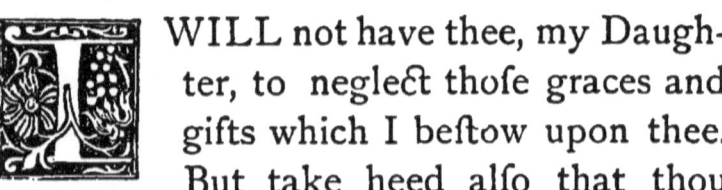

I WILL not have thee, my Daughter, to negleɛt thofe graces and gifts which I beſtow upon thee. But take heed alfo that thou doſt not feek thine own commendation in thefe graces of mine, that thou doſt not by them afcribe anything to thine own worthinefs, that thou art not puffed up with pride, that thou doft not boaft of them, glory in them, or defire to pleafe thine own felf by them, but employ them all wholly to my glory; remembering ever efpecially above all things, that of thyfelf thou art nothing, haft nothing, and art able to do nothing. And that whatfoever thou haft, thou haft received from me only.

2. And that I love not to have my gifts return unto me fruitlefs, and without doing of any good, but with gain and ufury, as I forewarned all men in the parable of talents, which I fpake of in the Gofpel. For as thine eye in thy body is not an eye only for itfelf, nor is placed there only for the ufe and benefit of itfelf, but to the end that it may help all the reft of the members to fee, fo what talents or gifts foever I have beftowed upon thee, I have not given them for thine own felf only, that thou fhouldft reap the whole fruit and benefit of them to thine own ufe, but I have placed thefe gifts or good things in thee, for the benefit of other members of my myftical body; that

by them thou mayeſt ſerve others, help others, and both gain and draw thy neighbours to the knowledge of my will, and the doing of my commandments. For peradventure I gave not them thoſe things which I gave thee, becauſe in thee I provided both for them and thyſelf alſo; as on the contrary part, I have to the ſame end withholden many graces from thee which I beſtowed upon them. For in theſe things which I beſtowed upon others, I had reſpect unto thee, and gave them not for themſelves only, but for thee in them, becauſe I beſtowed thoſe graces upon them for thy benefit.

2. I require, therefore, at thy hands, that thou employ my gifts to other men's welfare, and helpeſt other men moſt willingly, by them, as much as lieth in thy power. If thou canſt do ſomewhat which they can not, that ſo by this means one kind of charity remaining in you all, may make of many of you one body. And whatſoever this body hath, in one member, let him employ it to the benefit of the reſt. For every member ought to make one another

partaker of the gifts which every one of them receiveth, by reaſon of the union of the body and communion of charity which is amongſt them.

3. Let this conſideration of my will make thee, my Daughter, cheerful to ſerve thy neighbours, glad to bear their burdens, meek to ſuffer with them, gentle to comfort them, ready to ſuccour them, and willing to rejoice with them, that no envy at all, no contention, no emulation, no ſeeking to pleaſe thine own appetite, be found in thee, nor yet that any of theſe things may appear in thy fellows, but that there may remain between you perfect charity, and the communicating of my gifts one with another, as between the members of one body. For thou haſt nothing that is thine own. For what hast thou that thou haſt not received? Wherefore, thou haſt nothing, as I have ſaid, that is not mine, thou haſt nothing that is given to thyſelf alone; that is, thou haſt nothing that is given thee for thyſelf only, but all things whatſoever thou haſt received are committed to thy cuſtody, to be altogether employed for the benefit

of the whole body of my Church, and look unto it, for I will require an account at thy hands, how thou haft beftowed the fame.

4. Take heed, therefore, that thou be never carried away with fo profound a contemplation, or think thyfelf fo well and fo perfectly contented in being with me, but that (if either the corporal or fpiritual neceffity of thy neighbour do call thee away from it) thou be ready to forfake thine own confolation, the pleafure of thine own devotion, yea, and the fweet exercife or matter wherewith the confolation itfelf is nourifhed, and neglecting wholly to pleafe thyfelf, be willing to run in hafte to help thy neighbour for my fake. For this is perfect charity, not to feek thine own, but thy neighbour's benefit. And this charity is more acceptable unto me, and more profitable for thyfelf, than all the contemplation or devotion that thou canft ufe of thine own.

5. Moreover, remember always that in all thy actions, in all thy affections, and in all thofe things which either thou doft or makeft choice of, or fuffereft or feekeft to

avoid, I may be thy beginning, thy middle, and thy end. That whatsoever thou doest or leavest undone may be for my sake, and that in the following of this course thou seekest no other thing, but only my glory, and the fulfilling of my pleasure. For the deed is not so acceptable to me, in respect of itself, when thou dost succour or takest compassion upon thy neighbour; but thou art in doing hereof most acceptable in my sight because thou dost, for my sake, leave thyself; that is, because thou forsakest thine own welfare, and seekest to relieve thy neighbour's necessity. For if thou dost any thing for any other respect, whether it be for favour, friendship, or any special bond of kindred or familiarity, or for any gain or recompense which thou lookest to receive, I accept not of it, but reject it, although it be never so great and worthy an act. For I accept of no sacrifice that is offered up unto me, if it be not offered for my sake, only and wholly.

Chap. XXXI.

Of Poverty in Spirit.

O with all zeal and earneſtneſs as many good works as thou art able, hungering and thirſting after juſtice. And let no man ſeem unto thee more weak and imperfect, more void of all virtues, and more unworthy of my grace than thyſelf. Fix thine eyes always upon thine own defects, bewailing and lamenting that thou haſt ſo many imperfections, and wanteſt ſo many virtues. But remember withal that it is not thy duty to think and look into other men's manners, what virtues they have, what ways they walk, and how they behave themſelves towards me.

2. I know what I have given everybody; I know alſo what account is fit for me to require at everybody's hand. Imagine thyſelf in thine own eyes the baſeſt, vileſt, and wickedeſt of all men, and as it were merely nothing. Be aſhamed in my preſence, if thou heareſt any man praiſe thee, or ſhew

a good conceit of thee, and be sorry for it, because by it they do me injury, in that they think well of thee, which art so vile a soul, so unclean, so unthankful, and so full of offences against me.

3. Think thyself so vile, as that every man may lawfully and with just cause contemn and despise thee, and that thou mayest not think thyself injured, or else wronged at any time whensoever any seek to lay reproaches or afflictions upon thee. For thou oughtest to receive commendations or reproaches with an equal contentment in thy mind, and without any difference, but only in accounting thyself altogether unworthy of commendation, and most worthy of reproach. For as long as thou thinkest thyself to be wronged, as long as thou complainest, and dost believe that thou hast received any injury, thou art not clearly purged of self-love. For thou shouldst not, in truth, take anything for an injury, but that wrong which is done unto me.

4. Submit thyself, therefore, so wholly to my will and pleasure, as thou mayest be as

well content with evil as with good, with grief as with joy, which by an external accident doth happen to thee in this world, remaining always poor internally in thy fpirit, hungering and thirfting (as I faid) after juftice, and having a heart free from all earthly cogitations, and ready with all zeal and earneftnefs ever to do thofe things which agree beft with my good pleafure.

Chap. XXXII.

Of the Love of God.

MY Daughter, even as the hart defireth to come unto the fountains of water, fo let thy foul have a defire to come unto me, and thy mind be inflamed with the love and defire of me. He that is oppreffed with a vehement thirft, can think of nothing but of drink only; for whatfoever he doth, his burning thirft never forfaketh him, but ftill provoketh him with earneft cogitations and continual defires to have fome drink.

2. In like fort if thou didſt love me perfectly, if thou didſt long for me vehemently thou couldſt think of nothing elſe but how thou mighteſt come unto me, how thou mighteſt be united unto me. There would always remain in thee ſuch a hunger and thirſt after juſtice, that thou wouldſt never be fatisfied or contented with that which thou haſt done to mine honour, how great foever it were, but ever grieved and perplexed in thy mind, with thinking that the fame which thou haſt done already for my honour was nothing at all. Thou wouldſt always endeavour thyſelf to do better, thou wouldſt always thirſt to be more perfect, thy heart would ever burn with defire to be more nearly united unto me, to honour me more, and more fully to fulfil my will and good pleaſure.

3. They which are inflamed with an exceeding and an unmeaſurable love towards any man or woman, do loathe meat, drink, and all other things which feem either for delights to pleafe them or for neceſſary uſe to fuſtain their body, and pine away and grow fickly if they cannot enjoy their de-

fire, or if they find and perceive that they are not loved again. For they languish with mere love, and that maketh them that they can neither take any joy, nor receive any comfort, nor find any rest, except they may obtain that which they love.

4. Oh, my Daughter, thou oughtest to love me in this sort, that thou mightest find in me only joy and consolation, and without me in all places nothing but sorrow and affliction. If thou didst rightly love me as thou shouldst do, thou couldst not be in rest until thou didst possess me. For there would be a continual thirst, hunger, and desire burn within thy soul, not permitting thee to enjoy any quiet at all. Oh, that thou didst languish with such a kind of love towards me, or that, hating all other things, thou didst desire me only.

5. Oh, that thou didst present thy heart unto me quite weaned, and clearly delivered from all other love whatsoever, that I may still draw it after me, and both pierce it through and wound it to the bottom with my love. Oh, how happy shouldst

thou be if, being made quite befides thyfelf, and drunk with extremity of love towards me, thou didft defpife all things elfe, thou didft loathe all my creatures, and didft run only after me, crying unto me, I am wounded with thy charity. Thou oughteft, my Daughter, to be inflamed with fo fervent an affection towards me, as whofoever did come near unto thee, might perceive no other thing elfe, but only the heat of thine affection towards me, breathing out of thee; and whofoever did talk with thee might depart edified from thee, and warmed with the flames of that affection towards me which he found kindled in thy foul.

6. If, therefore, thou defireft to love me, thou muft love me with thy whole heart. I will not allow that thou fhouldft love me, and join with me any thing elfe befides me, that is, that thou fhouldft not love any thing for any other refpect but for my fake only. I look to be loved purely, and that thou canft never do but when thou loveft me for my own felf; that I only, and no other refpect whatfoever, be the caufe why thou

lovest me. I will also be loved with an infinite love, and with an unmeasurable desire; for thou shouldst never find in thy soul any end or measure in loving me, but although thou didst love me never so much, thou shouldst always desire to love me more. For my love is not restrained within any limits, but it is infinite, and without any bounds. It never thinketh itself satisfied, it can never be filled or contented with any quantity, though it be never so exceeding great, it will every day grow and increase to be more. For charity doth always increase, and what is charity but a good will?

7. As, therefore, a good will cannot be restrained within any limit, and as it is without all end, so is charity likewise. I know that thou hast a will to love me with all thy heart, and that thou desirest to love me as much thyself alone, as all my holy servants do, joining all their love together. This desire is good, if it proceed not from an appetite of desiring, in respect that thou wouldst be more excellent than they, and singular above them all, as though thou

To the Faithful Soul. 199

only couldſt love me as much as all they when all their love were put together. It is a good defire, I ſay, if it ſpringeth from pure and perfect charity only, and that thou doſt for my own fake, without any other refpect, defire me, love me, and wiſh ſtill to increafe in the love of me, and feek to love me as much alone, as it is poſſible for all other beings joined together. Have care, therefore, that this defire of thine proceed not of any appetite to be preferred before others, but only becaufe charity can never be fatisfied or filled, and that the greatnefs thereof maketh thee to think that how much foever thou loveſt me, is much inferior in thine eyes to that affection which thou doſt defire to carry towards me, and in no fort either anſwerable or agreeable to thy defire.

8. My love is no idle love, but it worketh great things where it is indeed. And where there is no defire, but an unaptnefs and unwillingnefs to do good works, there is no love without all doubt. And yet, notwithſtanding this, if thou wanteſt ability to do good works, be not therefore difcouraged,

my Daughter, or dejected in thy mind, for thy goodwill pleaseth me as much as if the work were done, and is as acceptable in my sight. I will not require an account of thee for that I have not bestowed upon thee. For it is not the multitude of works, but the greatness of love which delighteth me. Many good works, if they be presented unto me without charity, do pacify me no whit at all. For what is chaff to me without wheat? To whomsoever thou dost offer wheat, which is love, offer him also chaff, which is works.

9. For although I regard not works without love, yet I will have good regard of thy love without works, so as thou be hindered by disability, necessity, obedience, or any other lawful impediment, in such sort, as thou art not able to do good works. For then, as I have said, I accept of thy good will. But where power wanteth not, if love remain, it doth extend itself, and exercise itself towards me, and for my sake towards her neighbour. For I have placed him as a companion with thee in my stead, that whatsoever thou wouldst bestow upon

me, and cannot, thou mayeſt beſtow upon him. And that thou mayeſt do it the more willingly, I have promiſed that I will accept as well at thy hands, and reward as largely, any thing that thou doſt towards thy neighbour as if thou hadſt done it to myſelf. For if thou haſt charity, it worketh ſo in thee, as thou loveſt him for my ſake, thou beholdeſt me in him, thou ſerveſt me in him, thou doeſt me benefits in him, thou doſt bear and ſuffer with me in him, and if he offend thee, thou doſt forgive him for my ſake.

10. And for this cauſe I gave him unto thee in my ſtead, that thou mayeſt beſtow theſe good turns upon him, as time and place ſerveth, and as thou haſt opportunity offered by me to do the ſame. For thou muſt not forget that which I repeated before, how charity is not to be meaſured or eſteemed by the multitude of works, but by the greatneſs and ſincerity of thy affection, that is, by the inward devotion of thy mind, joined with a pure, chaſte, and internal diſpoſition, inclination, and intention of thy will, which, the more ready, prompt, fervent,

and desirous it is to obey me, honour me, and please me, and the more that she renounceth her own self, in seeking to please me purely, without any other respect, and to prefer me before all other creatures, the more she is drawn to love me, and the brighter she doth shine in all good works.

11. Oh, if the children of men did know how much it pleaseth me to dwell in such a soul, how gladly I do offer myself unto her which desireth me only, how bountifully I do pour myself into such a heart as doth seek me only with a pure intention, being withdrawn and free both from the love of herself and of any other creature besides, desiring me fervently, respecting me wholly, staying for me patiently, and refusing to be comforted with any other thing but with me only. Nay, such a heart as I speak of will not desire to be comforted by me, because she thinketh herself unworthy to receive any consolation from me, but desireth only to be satisfied with having my good will and pleasure fulfilled in her. For she only desireth to do, to suffer, and to be in no other sort than agreeth with my pleasure;

and then, although such a heart neither desireth comfort, nor any thing else, which is without me, yet I do reward and enrich her with all blessings and benefits.

12. For there can be nothing wanting in any creature, neither can there be any thing forsaken for the love of me, that is so good but that there shall be found in me things instead of them, a hundred times better, purer, sweeter, pleasanter, and more delightful than they were. For whether it be beauty, sweetness, pleasantness, delight, love, truth, consolation, the continual enjoying of such things as men do like, riches, glory, power, and innumerable other things of the same sort, which either may bring delights to them or procure desire to them; all these things are after an infinite manner more excellent, and more perfect in me, than in any creature whatsoever.

13. Oh, my Daughter, the smallest consolation which thou feelest by the presence of my goodness in thy soul doth surmount all the delights of the world, and the pleasure that can be taken in any creature whatsoever. Yea, all other delights being com-

pared with it, do feem bitter and unpleafant. Wherefore, if things were meafured by a true and juft account, it could not be but that men would love me better than themfelves, or any other creature. But now (it is a lamentable thing to be fpoken) men do leave me, who am their greateft good; they defpife my goodnefs. Nay, which is more, they forfake their own true and only happinefs, and fall to love themfelves, to delight in the world, from whence all difquietnefs of mind and all other mifchiefs do proceed.

14. Alas! why are miferable men so far deceived? If they delight in love, why love they not me, whofe love is chafte, pure, holy, and fimple; who am an object always offered to their eyes, of infinite amiablenefs, being effentially good in myfelf, being a pure good, unmixed, being the chiefeft and fovereign good, where the reward of love alfo is unfpeakable delight, and moft bleffed eternity? Whereas the love of the world, on the contrary part, doth breed nothing in thy foul but unquietnefs, bitternefs, diftraction, repentance, and heavinefs. Leave thou, therefore, and contemn all worldly

things, and defire me only, being united unto me with all thy foul, with all thy heart, and with all thy will. For as long as thou doft addict thyfelf to the love of creatures, thou fhalt find that which is in creatures; that is, thou fhalt be defiled and difquieted with corrupt and unclean delights, and yet, befides that, be never fatiffied or contented. And thou fhalt alfo be polluted with impure imaginations, and be diftracted with fundry cogitations, that are lewd and wicked. But I do recollect that heart, which feeketh to be joined with me, and I unite it faft unto me, procuring in it by my means all peace, quietnefs, and all tranquillity of confcience.

15. Thou oughteft continually to entreat me, and without ceafing to pray unto me, that thou mayeft after this fort forfake the world, renounce the love of all my creatures, and be wholly converted unto me, and inwardly dedicated in thy foul to my fervice. For no man can beftow this grace on thee, neither canft thou obtain it by any other means but by me only. Wherefore thou muft always with great regard obferve

the internal infpirations of my grace, thou muft follow my counfel, obey my exhortations, and commit thyfelf altogether to my providence. My infpirations do never difagree from the holy Scripture, nor from the obedience which thou muft carry to thy Superiors. Therefore, if thou fubmitteft thyfelf unto them, and relieft in no refpect upon thine own felf, thou art fure to walk in all fimplicity and purity of heart.

16. Love is an incomparable treafure, and therefore I fhould be the ftore-houfe of the fame, and it fhould never be laid up but in me only. Oh, my Daughter, where thy treafure is, there is thy heart alfo. If, then, thou wilt know what thou loveft, mark what thou doft ofteneft think upon, what thou doft with greateft delight and willingnefs hearken unto, what thou doft moft fervently defire, what thou doft inwardly in thine own appetite moft feek, and bend thyfelf unto; for that is, without all doubt, thy treafure, and therein thou findeft fweeteft reft, moft quiet, and greateft contentment. And both of them is thy treafure, both the thing which thou loveft and the

love wherewith thou loveſt the ſame. But ſee into how great miſery, how great unthankfulneſs, and how great infelicity men do fall by this means; for they do purchaſe to themſelves hell fire, with the expenſe of incomparable treaſure, which is love. For if men contemning me, fall to love corrupt, unclean, and frail things, ſuch as will quickly periſh; they do with the ſame love which they beſtow upon them procure unto themſelves eternal torment. Let all my friends, therefore, bewail and lament this ſtrange and unnatural kind of dealing, that I am clean thruſt out of the heart of man, for whom I offered up myſelf in ſacrifice, and whoſe ſalvation I did buy with my precious blood; and that another which is mine enemy, doth poſſeſs it, and doth poſſeſs it only to this end, that he may draw them with him into eternal deſtruction, into endleſs miſery, and into unquenchable fire.

Chap. XXXIII.
Of the Praife of God.

BE always inflamed, my Daughter, with a defire to praife me, to love me, to honour me, and to pleafe me from the bottom of thy heart altogether, and by all the means that thou art able, and in fuch moft perfect fort as I require at thy hands. Carry always in thy heart fo great a reverence, fo great a fear, fo great a care, fo great a love and affection towards me, and for me, as thou mayeft never do any thing to difpleafe or offend me. And although it ought to be thy greateft care, thy chiefeft fear, and thy fpecial labour, not to do any thing thyfelf, or to give any occafion by thine own negligence, that any thing fhould be done to offend me; yet, neverthelefs, thou oughteft alfo to take as much care as lieth in thee for others, that I be not by them difhonoured or offended, or that they do break my will and commandment. And thou oughteft to do this with a pure intention of mere charity, for my fake, without any other refpect.

2. For there should ever abound in thy heart a most faithful, fervent, and devout love of me, which should continually flow with forcible streams every day nearer and nearer towards me, and it should carry thee with so great violence, and run over in such exceeding abundance, as it should make thee most ready and desirous to do all things that may be for my glory, and for the fulfilling of my pleasure; and it should possess thee in such sort as thou shouldst desire nothing so much as to be clearly delivered, quite discharged, and altogether weaned from all love, respect, desire, or inclination towards thyself, or any of my creatures, and to keep thyself in the same state, pure, clean, chaste, and unspotted to me only, desiring me with a pure intention, and no other thing; that by this means I may have my will, without any impediment, freely and wholly fulfilled in thee, and by thee, and that I only may possess thee, and that there may be no space or division between thee and me, but that thou mayest be close united unto me, having renounced and forsaken all love, both of thyself and any other creature.

3. Desire likewise that my will may be done in all things, and with all men, and that all men may know me, love me, honour me, worship me, and serve me. Thou wouldst rather choose to suffer ten deaths (if thou wert a faithful spouse unto me) than once to consent to any sin, although it were but venial. For albeit it is not likely that thou canst long stand in perfection without venial sin, yet thou must not in any wise, willingly or of set purpose, yield to any venial sin, but thou must ever be fully resolved in thine own will never to sin again. And thou must fix and settle this will of thine, in the hope of my grace, and not upon any confidence in thine own ability.

4. I do ever please and delight him that loveth me, and all my works and judgments seem sweet and pleasant to him, and he never ceaseth to praise me for them. He that loveth me need not study to find somewhat for which he might praise me, for the love which he beareth me will shew unto him what may or ought to be praised in me. And to praise me is no other thing

but, by loving me, to think upon me; and by honouring of me, to wonder at my works; and by wondering at my works, to defire that all men fhould extol, magnify, and love me. My praife doth lighten his heart which loveth me with a pure affection, it doth rejoice his fpirit, it driveth away all heavinefs from him, and withal it is a fafe protection for him, both in profperity and adverfity.

5. Whofoever fpendeth his time in praifing of me, it maketh him with all fortitude of mind to contemn all the mifchief that the fubtlety of man or the devil can practife againft him. Oh, how delightful a thing is it to my angels to hear the fweet fongs of them which do continually praife me (although it be much more delightful unto them to affift their pure hearts, and to help them in fetting forth of my praife) for they fee men upon earth do imitate by this means the order of the celeftial companies in heaven, as though they had received here the earneft-penny, or elfe fome fenfible feeling of eternal happinefs, which is only a continual praifing and magnifying

of my name. For there is nothing that doth fo lively refemble the ftate of the bleffed happinefs in the world to come, as the cheerful and delightful voice of thofe which do praife my name.

6. And touching myfelf, I am of fo great majefty and omnipotency, as I ftand in need of no praife, and no praife can make me more glorious than I am already, neither is any creature able to praife and magnify me as I do deferve. Wherefore thou oughteft to think thyfelf moft unworthy to praife me; neverthelefs, defire yet to praife me, that thou mayeft know, and it may appear manifeft unto thee, how that all human praife is nothing in refpect of my worthinefs, and how I am far greater than all the praife that can be given me, and how all creatures, when they have praifed me as much as they are able, have done it much inferior to that I am worthy of, and therefore muft yield that they are altogether infufficient to praife me. And although that I declare unto thee how that every creature muft give this praife to me, yet I would have thee efpecially to imprint

this leffon in thy mind, that although thou doft endeavour never fo much to praife me (which thou oughteft at all times to do with all thy force) yet thou fhouldft think that thou hadft done nothing at all.

7. I will tell thee, my Daughter, what kind of praife doth pleafe me—vocal praife. Although I would have thee always to ufe it, and with thy voice to perform it, whenfoever thou art commanded by the precept of my Church to fay or fing anything, yet I muft needs tell thee that it doth not pleafe me fo much as that internal praife which confifteth in the fpirit. A profound contemplation and perfect knowledge of thine own bafenefs, a confideration of thine own weaknefs, how thou art of thyfelf merely nothing, and a modeft fhame procured by the means of thy unworthinefs before my Majefty, is a moft fweet fmelling facrifice, and a moft delightful praife unto me. Becaufe thou fhalt be brought by it, with a fhame-faced kind of modefty, continually to look into and to defpife, in my glorious prefence, thine own vilenefs, deformednefs, unthankfulnefs, wretchednefs

and misery, and be also moved to acknowledge how thou art of thyself merely nothing, and therefore be desirous to humble and subject thyself before me and every one of my creatures, and to be willing, or rather to wish to be in respect of thine own baseness, contemned, and trodden under them all. Such a contrite and humbled heart I can never despise; yea, the sorrowful groans of such a heart, are a much sweeter and worthier sacrifice unto me than a huge heap of many words and a tedious multitude of vocal prayers only.

8. Moreover, thou dost then likewise truly and rightly praise me when I am as acceptable unto thee for sending adversity as prosperity, and when thou givest me as many thanks, and remainest as devoutly and zealously affected towards me in thine own will, for the one as for the other. It is not also the least praise that thou mayest yield me to beware of sin, to take great pains in seeking after virtue, to thirst for the honouring and extolling of my name, and to seek only for the fulfilling of my pleasure and the setting forth of my glory.

Besides this, it is a much purer kind of praise, and more acceptable unto me than any vocal praise, to keep thy heart undefiled, pure, and free from all vicious affections, from all slothful humours, from all heaviness, unwillingness, and frowardness in thy soul, and to cleave unto me only in all peace, tranquillity, and silence of thy spirit.

9. What motion soever thou feelest within thee, my Daughter, what outward accident soever doth happen unto thee, presently repair unto me with thy heart wholly converted and submitted unto my will, and wish that it may be turned by my grace to my greatest glory and highest praise. By doing after this sort, all things that happen unto thee shall be for the furtherance of thy salvation, and even nature itself by this virtuous custom shall be changed into grace. Wherefore, if thou findest within thyself any mischievous attempts of the devil, any filthy temptations or horrible blasphemies, or dost sensibly perceive in thy soul the motion of any odious temptation whatsoever, endeavour thou to win some profit or benefit to

thy foul by the fame means whereby thine enemy feeketh to do thee a mifchief, and account it a benefit for thy foul, if it may bring thee to praife and glorify me.

10. As foon, therefore, as thou feeleft any of thefe temptations, come prefently unto me, and fay: O Lord, my God, as often as I feel this temptation, as often as it cometh into my mind, fo often do I glorify Thee, with the praifes of the whole court of heaven, and fo often do I adore Thee, to the confufion of this wicked fpirit which affaulteth me, and to the honour and glory of Thy name. And in his place I offer unto Thee infinite praifes, which he is not able to do. If it be a grievous temptation which thou feeleft, fay : O moft merciful God, although it be very troublefome which I fuffer, yet I will willingly endure it for the love of Thee only, and for Thy honour ; and if it may be to Thy greater honour that I fhould fuffer greater and more grievous temptations than this is, behold, I offer myfelf ready with all my heart to do it. Let nothing, O merciful God, feem fo troublefome unto me, but that I may

To the Faithful Soul.

defire above all things to fuftain any thing that may be for the glory of Thy name.

11. If thou feeleft any cogitation in thy foul of beautiful, delightful, or precious things, fay: O, moft fweet God, this proceedeth from Thee, which art moft goodly, moft beautiful, moft fweet, moft to be defired, and moft worthy to be embraced, becaufe Thou art the greateft good. If it be Thy pleafure, I will willingly want all Thy creatures, I will willingly forfake all confolation, that Thou only mayeft remain in my heart, and mayeft wholly poffefs me, which art moft beautiful, and far more beautiful than all the faireft things befides Thee; which art moft fweet, and far more fweet than all the beft and fweeteft things befides Thee; which art moft to be defired, and above all to be beloved, becaufe Thou art far more amiable and precious than all the moft precious and moft amiable things befides Thee.

12. Likewife, if thou either heareft or feeft any number affembled together, or as often as thou beholdeft any exceeding beautiful thing or great multitude of people,

say so often in the day to thyself: O most good and most amiable Lord, O Almighty and eternal God, let thousand thousands of the armies of celestial spirits praise Thee out of me, and let ten thousand hundred thousand of those that stand before Thee extol and magnify Thy name out of me and for me, and let all the worthy supplications of Thy Blessed Saints make intercession unto Thee for me, and let the beauty of every one of Thy creatures, and the sweet harmony of them altogether, glorify Thee out of me for ever, and world without end.

Chap. XXXIV.

Of the Exercise of the Love and Praise of God.

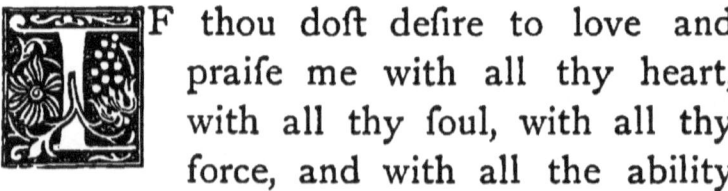F thou dost desire to love and praise me with all thy heart, with all thy soul, with all thy force, and with all the ability that doth rest in thee, and desirest to persevere in the loving of me to the end, thou must of necessity have some exercises

of love, whereby thou mayeſt nouriſh it, kindle it, increaſe and maintain it. And for this cauſe keep thy mind free, withdrawn, weaned, and clearly delivered from the love of my creatures, and from all internal occupation of thy mind or buſineſs about them, and from all care and trouble of this preſent world, by lifting it up unto me with continual, vehement, and ſcalding ſighs, and enflamed prayers, burning with all zeal, and by aſpiring inceſſantly with moſt fervent deſire to come unto me; that is to ſay, by deſiring to love me moſt ardently, moſt perfectly, moſt vehemently, moſt faithfully, and withal continually, yea and thirſting alſo to pleaſe me in all reſpects, to praiſe me with all zeal, with all fidelity, and with all the ſufficiency that is in thy power, and to fulfil my will abſolutely and perfectly in all things.

2. To conclude, thou muſt always have a deſire to ſee me, who am moſt beautiful; to poſſeſs me, who am moſt bleſſed; and to be with me, who only am able to grant thee happineſs, being the fountain from whom all felicity doth proceed, in whom all

sweetness doth consist, and by whom all goodness must be granted. For I am of all things the sweetest, the best, and the happiest, yea, true happiness itself. Cleave, therefore, always to me, and be never separated from me. Have ever somewhat in thy mind which thou mayest meditate upon, and which may enflame thee with the love of me, whereby thou mayest think of my sweetness and goodness, and, by wondering at it, magnify and praise my name. Or else, on the contrary part, meditate upon somewhat which may move thee to bewail, lament, accuse, and reprehend thyself for thy vileness, baseness, weakness, infirmity, inconstancy, or unthankfulness, or else that may procure thee suffering, even with sorrow in thy soul, from the bottom of thy heart, with those that be afflicted and dead, to make supplications unto me for them, and for my universal Church. Moreover, whatsoever thou art to do, or what thing soever thou hast to think or consider of, think of them first with me, receive counsel touching them first from me, and discourse of them first with me, that thou mayeſt be brought by this cuſtom always, and at all times (whether thou beeſt alone or in the company of others), to talk with me, and to keep thy heart ſtill lifted up unto me, either by prayer or elſe by praiſing of my name.

3. Do whatſoever belongeth to my honour; whatſoever thou knoweſt will content me or is my will, that thou ſhouldſt perform with an unſpeakable thirſt to pleaſe me; and with an inſatiable deſire to honour me, and labour thus by all the means thou mayeſt, and endeavour with thy help, with thy counſel, with thy travail, and by all the other means that do lie in thy power to advance my glory, that my name may be praiſed both by thyſelf and others, and that my will may be fulfilled in all my creatures. But in the meantime, notwithſtanding, while thy outward man is thus occupied abroad, let thy inward man remain quietly with me, for thou muſt in no wiſe give thyſelf ſo much to external buſineſs, as that thy mind ſhould be diſtracted and run wandering after ſundry cogitations, and that thou ſhouldſt draw by this means

into thy foul many fond imaginations and vain fancies. But rather whilſt thy outward man is buſied, be thou recollected in thy ſpirit, and gathered cloſe together in thy ſoul, that it being united unto me, thou mayeſt ever internally remain with me.

4. And when thou haſt learned this leſſon, when thou haſt accuſtomed thyſelf to this courſe, no external buſineſs ſhall hinder thee no external act ſhall hurt or withhold thee (eſpecially if it be a good and modeſt one) from the mental exerciſe of the love of me. But thou ſhalt ſpeak unto me, or rather be in thy ſoul peaceably united unto me, as well at that time as at any other, ſo long as thou doſt not (as I have ſaid) entangle thy mind with thinking of vain and tranſitory things, nor remaineſt drowned in the cogitations of thoſe external buſineſſes which thou practiceſt in this world. For as long as thou haſt a will to keep thy heart free from the love of all creatures, there is no creature that can win or withdraw thee from me (although in thy outward man thou be troubled with never ſo many buſineſſes, nor occupied with never

so many actions), if thou imprinteſt not the forms, the repreſentations, the love or delight of theſe things internally in thy mind.

5. Wherefore, never complain that external good works are an impediment unto thee in thy loving of me, or in the exerciſe of thy love towards me. For theſe things do not hinder thee (as thou doſt imagine, and conceive in thy mind), but thy inordinate affection, thy want of diſcretion, thy infirmity, and thy evil inclination, are thoſe things which do hinder thee, becauſe thou haſt not as yet fully mortified them all, for theſe do make thee not only outwardly, but alſo inwardly, buſied and occupied with thinking of my creatures. Moreover, thy mind being more and more diſtracted, divided, and made more wandering by the multitude of theſe conceits, is far from being able to cleave unto me, nay, it cannot continue conſtant or quiet within itſelf. But be, notwithſtanding, no whit diſcouraged, if, in reſpect of brotherly charity, or of ſhewing thine obedience, thou art enforced sometimes to be occupied and diſquieted in thine inward man for my ſake. For I can

quickly amend whereinsoever thou hast faulted for my sake, and repair it again, with such advantage and gain unto thee, that thou shalt be afterwards so much the nearer and with greater delight united unto me, as thou didst think thyself before farther estranged from me.

6. But if thou find thy mind so much distracted and alienated from me, as thou canst neither recollect it again nor yet return and lift it up unto me, think not that it wandered thus in respect of that charity which thou didst shew merely for my sake; but that thine own wicked inclination hath polluted thee, and that there was somewhat hidden within thee which moved thee to this, whereof I was neither the Author nor occasion, neither yet was it any way procured by my means. Thou wert not belike circumspect and watchful enough, and therefore thou didst suffer some human infirmity. But remain not long estranged or alienated from me, for I am always ready to receive thee again into my favour.

7. Let thy mind, therefore, be ever occupied in holy desires, that no moment may

pafs thee wherein thou doft not wound me and feek to pierce my heart with the fiery darts of thy inflamed defires. Be affured, my Daughter, that thou canft defire nothing at my hands in vain. For if thou doft defire me thou fhalt find me, but if I do withdraw and hide myfelf from thee for a time, I do it for thy fake and thy benefit. For I cannot choofe but grant my prefence to thofe that call upon me and defire me. I do ftir up thefe defires in thee, I infpire thy heart with thefe motions, and therefore be fure that I will alfo hearken to thy petitions and hear thy prayers. For although it fhould fo fall out by the means of my providence, as thou fhouldft remain unheard by me to the hour of thy death, yet it is impoffible that I fhould not at all hear a devout prayer, but I will even at that inftant render thee an hundred fold for thy long forbearing. Thou fhalt then perceive that I will give thee for one petition a thoufand ; thou fhalt then find that thou art heard at my hands, when thou canft never again lofe the benefit thereof.

8. But in all thy prayers let this be thy

chiefest petition, to defire at my hands that thou mayest poffefs me. For what is more holy, what is more for my glory, than to defire me above all things, and before all things? Pray, therefore, always only for a naked, a pure, a moft chafte, a moft perfect, a moft earneft, a moft watchful, and a moft faithful charity towards me, whereby both thyfelf and all other reafonable creatures may cleave unto me with a refolute mind and with fuch a firm intention, as no accident whatfoever fhall be ever able to withdraw you from me. .

Chap. XXXV.

Of the Transformation of Man.

IF thou wilt obtain me wholly, O Soul, thou muft of neceffity altogether forfake thyfelf, and altogether caft off thyfelf. Thou muft fubmit and refign over thyfelf to extreme poverty, and the want of all temporal commodities and confolations, for obtaining of me, who am the chiefeft and greateft good. Comfort thyself, therefore, and be not dismayed, though thou be deprived of all human consolation, and though thou want all human friendship, favour, and succour whatsoever.

2. Consider how a stout soldier, not regarding his friends, his country, his wife, his children, his quiet rest, and his commodity at home, doth forsake them all, and being a stranger in a foreign land, doth there daily offer his life to dangerous labours, to painful journeys, to continual watching, and to sundry miseries and perils, that he may obtain riches and win honour. In this sort must thou, forsaking all things, be spoiled and made poor, and deprived of all comfort, and of all my creatures whatsoever, that nothing may remain in thee wherein thou mayest find any quiet, or that thou mayest possess but me only. Moreover, thou must exclude and banish from thyself the forms, impressions, and memory of all things, and thou must cleanse and purge thy mind of them all, and carry about with thee the image of me only imprinted in thy heart, wheresoever thou becomest, and

howsoever thou art, either alone by thyself or in company of others.

3. Thou muſt alſo, whether thou eateſt or drinkeſt, ſleepeſt or wakeſt, ſpeakeſt or be ſilent, always look into me, as a pure glaſs and moſt perfect pattern for thee to imitate, that thou mayeſt direct thy courſe of life and transform thyſelf according to the virtues and manner of my life. If thou eateſt, dip every morſel in my wounds. If thou drinkeſt, take the warm blood out of my wounds, which will breathe charity into thee. If thou ſpeakeſt, look upon me who heareth thy words, and beware that thou ſpeakeſt nothing that is uncomely or may diſpleaſe me. If thou holdeſt thy peace, hearken unto me who do ſpeak to thee, and ſearch out with all diligence and care what is my perfect will and good pleaſure. If thou ſleepeſt, lean and repoſe thyſelf upon my heart, applying thy mouth to the gaping wound of my ſacred heart, and ſuck my grace thereby into thy ſpirit, and breathe again unto me, by ſending a ſweet ſmelling ſacrifice out of it, the marrow and precious treaſure of thy heart.

To the Faithful Soul. 229

4. To be short, wheresoever thou be, govern and direct thyself according to that most notable, most worthy, and most perfect pattern, which thou beholdest in the course of my life. Look into and desire earnestly, with all zeal and affection, to imitate my most modest and most lowly humility, my most courteous affability, my most sweet meekness, my most enduring patience, my most pure chastity, my most abundant piety, my most faithful providence, my most merciful compassion, and my most fervent-burning, exceeding and incomprehensible charity. Imprint the lively image of these things in thy soul, fill thy mind wholly with it, and by the means thereof banish altogether from thy mind all the forms and imaginations of all other things whatsoever. I will not have thee to be without the impression or the representation of something in thy heart, neither yet will I have thee seek before thy time to fly higher than this.

5. Wherefore rest thou quietly in the mean space, in beholding the image of my humanity and Passion, until I do raise thee

up to a higher dignity, where thou shalt not feel these motions, but be wholly and clearly delivered from any impression or imagination, and be free from all exercise and action, and remain in all peace and quietness, having clean forsaken thyself and thine own appetite. In the meantime, therefore, meditate how I am always present with thee, and how I do look and pierce into the closest corners of thy soul, and into the deepest secrets of thy heart, and do not only meditate upon it, but learn also to have a sensible feeling of my presence, whereby I do always behold thee, always mark thee, always look into thee, and always both fully know thee and perfectly understand thy greatest secrets.

6. Learn to conceive how I am without all limitation, not possible to be circumscribed within any bounds; how I am an unchangeable, an eternal, an unspeakable, and an incomprehensible light; how I am best worthy to be beloved; how I only deserve to be desired; and how I am wholly pure and sincere, not stained with the least evil or smallest imperfection. Likewise,

how I am wholly good, in whom there is nothing but it is to be beloved, and able to delight all that feek me ; how I am wholly moſt faithful, wholly moſt merciful, and always ready moſt abundantly to communicate myſelf with the children of men. To conclude, learn to know how I am a moſt conſtant and faithful lover, a moſt fweet comforter, a moſt mighty protector, and a moſt rich and bountiful rewarder of all thofe that bear me good will, of all thofe that love me, and of all thofe that hope in me, and how I am able to bring more delight unto their fouls, than all other things that can be defired. For I never procure loathefomenefs in them, but I fatisfy all their defires, and by fatisfying them I daily more and more increafe their defires in them. Let this perfect image of me wholly poffefs thy mind, and imprint it fo deeply therein that thou mayeſt not confent in thy will to the meditation of any other fancies, but prefently banifh them from thee as foon as they begin to enter into thee.

7. Take heed that thou do not receive

them within thy soul, but being free from them, remain united to me only, in all internal solitariness, in all internal quietness, and in all internal peace and tranquillity, waiting for me continually, most desirously, and without ceasing, that thou mayest repose thyself in all things upon me, that thou mayest follow me, and that thou mayest submit thyself unto any thing whatsoever that I will have thee either to do or suffer, yea, unto whatsoever I will have done in thee, or with thee. Thou oughtest so clearly to renounce thyself, that is, all love of thyself, and all proper inclination to follow thine own will, as that nothing may be able to move thy reasonable and intellectual soul, being now, as it were, quite alienated and separated from thy body. And that it may seem all one unto her, whether her external or sensible man be praised or discommended, be afflicted or comforted, and that she may look upon him, as it were, afar off, being clean divided from him, and wholly united and joined unto me.

8. To obtain this separation of thyself from the following of thine own appetite,

and the love of any creature, thou muſt of neceſſity, as I warned thee before, have great watch over thyſelf, and ſtraightly obſerve by what means thou mayeſt ſooneſt find out and diſcern what lieth hidden in thy ſecret thoughts, what moveth thee, what draweth thee, what enticeth thee, what poſſeſſeth thee, what reigneth in thee; to conclude, what thou loveſt, or inclineſt thyſelf unto, whether it be thyſelf, or any other creature, or me. And thou muſt thruſt preſently out of thy mind whatſoever thou findeſt there, if it be not myſelf, or anything whereof I am not the cauſe; for thou art then become ſubject to that thing which poſſeſſeth thee, when it hath gotten a full intereſt and propriety in thee.

9. And I, for mine own part, will never conſent to be beloved with a companion, but I look for thy whole love, and I deſire to remain alone peaceably in thee. Therefore, except thou ſeekeſt me only, thou ſhalt never perfectly find me, and if thou wilt enjoy me, baniſh all creatures from thee, ſuffer no diviſion, no impediment, no ſeparation to remain between thee and me.

Let all creatures be banished from thee, but only such as are for thy mere and necessary use; let them have no interest or place in thee; let them not possess thy heart, that thou mayest keep thyself free and pure unto me from them all, and mayest wholly submit thyself unto me, and be ready to be disposed in all such sorts as it shall be my pleasure.

10. Whatsoever shall happen, it is enough for thee that thou knowest it, and findest that it hath happened. Trouble thyself no farther with thinking of it, neither suffer it to stay within thee, or to leave any memory or impression thereof in thy soul. But rely upon me, and commit all thy cares unto me; pass and fly over the multitude, the variety, and the mutability of these cogitations, and never fix or settle thy heart but in me only. Seek, therefore, me only, and no more but me in all things, which am one in all and all in all, and wait patiently with long-suffering till thou findest me, yea, be content to stay and wait for me again and again, and never be weary of waiting till thou findest me, reposing thyself upon my

goodnefs, and upon my moft wife providence, full of all love towards thee, with a ftrong faith and an affured truft therein. When I ftay my coming, expect me patiently, for I will come at the laft without doubt. Be free and altogether weaned in this fort, O Soul, from all thine own defire; be feparated wholly from all love and delights in creatures; be alienated from all fancies and imaginations, and cleave wholly unto me in fimplicity and nakednefs of heart. Offer thyfelf to be poffeffed by me, and forfake clean thine own will, that thou mayeft rejoice with me in all eternity, where there are neither things paft nor things to come, but all things prefent.

11. Afpire always, and earneftly defire to obtain this even now, and forfake both thyfelf and all other things, that is, thy body and fenfuality, and have thine eye fo fixed upon eternity in this prefent world as if thou wert quite feparated from it, and clearly delivered out of it, beholding all the things in this world afar off, as thofe things which thou haft wholly forfaken, and from which thou haft clearly weaned thyfelf.

Think that thou art alone with me, and that I am with thee, and as if there were no other creature prefent with thee. Whatfoever thou feeleft befides me, make no account of it, becaufe it is in truth nothing worth being without me, and no creature fhall hurt thee as long as thou receive not within thy heart the fancies and imaginations of any thing, nor yet feel any cares or affections within thy foul.

THE CONCLUSION.

DELIVER thefe exhortations unto thee, as to my Daughter and Spoufe, O Soul, and as a rule to inftruct thee how thou fhouldft put off the old man, and walk hereafter in newnefs of fpirit, and how thou fhouldft daily bend and endeavour thyfelf, with all thy force, to grow to more perfection. Therefore, as often as, by reading over thefe things, thou findeft that thou haft not obferved all in fuch fort as I have

commanded thee, or that thou haſt faulted in ſome little part thereof, ſo often ſtill renew thy good intention, by ſtirring up a new fervour of zeal in thee. And although I give thee theſe to read, yet I deſire, notwithſtanding, that the ears of thy heart ſhould always be open to my inſpirations, whereby thou mayeſt not only outwardly read them, but inwardly hear theſe leſſons from me.

13. And the reaſon why I would have theſe my written inſpirations laid before thine eyes, is becauſe thou art for the moſt part delighted with vain letters and meſſages from thy friends, which do procure in thy heart nothing but diſtraction, an unſavoury kind of diſquiet, and a perilous kind of darkneſs. Therefore, when thou haſt contemned theſe vanities, and forſaken them quite, I have given thee theſe wholeſome inſtructions, that thou mighteſt have ſome good thing for me to read, and to occupy thy mind withal. And that thou mighteſt by the conſideration of them, and for the love of me, deſpiſe all other things which ſeek to pollute thy

heart. And the more that I, who am thy Spouse, and gave thee these lessons, O Soul, ought to be beloved, the more acceptable ought this instruction to be unto thee, which proceeded from me, that am not only worthy to be beloved, but most worthy of all things to be beloved, and deserve above all things most to be desired, yea, and ought before all things most to please and delight thee.

14. I would have thee also the more faithfully to observe these precepts, seeing all these things which I have delivered unto thee are not to delight a carnal and worldly heart but a spiritual, and such an one as is devout towards me, and seeing they do not please the ears with picked phrases and trifling words, but they feed the loving soul with truth and wholesome counsel. It remaineth only now to warn thee, that thou be watchful and diligent, for I stand at the door of thy heart and knock. Open thy heart, therefore, unto me, O, my Sister, O my Spouse, give me thy heart, and desire me only, seeing I do so much desire thee. But assure thyself of this one thing, thou canst

never receive me as long as thou loveſt any thing beſides me. Thou canſt never have me as long as thou haſt any thing of thyſelf without me. Thou canſt never enjoy me as long as thou poſſeſſeſt thyſelf. Go, therefore, out of thyſelf, and forſake thyſelf, that I only may poſſeſs thee, and that thou only mayeſt poſſeſs me. This is a ſhort time which is preſent, but that which followeth is without all limitation of time and eternal, without any end.

15. Be watchful, therefore, my Daughter. I do once again exhort thee, receive me for thy husband, O Soul, O Daughter, O Spouſe, and ſhew thyſelf in all purity, without all hypocriſy or diſſimulation, a ſpouſe worthy of me. Love me, who am thy Lord and Redeemer, think of me, take heed to thyſelf, have conſideration of thine own eſtate. Cleave unto me, and perſevere with me to the end. Live happily henceforth in me, and ſo I bid thee farewell.

THE INSTRUCTIONS:

That follow are very fit and profitable for all Men. They are divided into two rules, and may either be called Rules of Direction for Man's Life, or else the Fraternity of the Disciples of Christ, that is to say, of such as desire to imitate the life of Christ, and seek to live after the rule of the Gospel, and do study with all their endeavour to attain to the Perfection of Charity.

JESUS CHRIST, who was made man for your sakes, did preach unto the world in times past, and did deliver them one rule of life by my Gospel, for the salvation of them all; he that believeth it can never err, and he that observeth it can never perish. For it only is sufficient alone for the salvation of man's soul, being well observed, and it instructeth a man fully in all virtue and perfection.

2. Wherefore, if men did live after that rule, there were no need of the rules of Monks, there were no need of any fraternities, or affociations, and companies of men that live under one rule and order, there were no need of any Canons whatfoever, feeing that they which did live purely and fincerely, after the rules of my Gofpel, needed no other thing to inftruct them in all perfection. But after that men forfook the rule of my Gofpel, and every man did only think upon his own proper commodity according to the nature of men, it came then to pafs, not without my counfel and the direction of my fpirit, that many of my faints did devife fundry means whereby they might root out of men's minds the love of the world and of themfelves, which made them quite forfake me, and grow cold in the zeal of my Gofpel and my honour, and befides that they might reftore unto the world a perfect courfe of life, how to obferve my Gofpel and commandments.

3. Therefore, many of them have fet down certain rules how to keep under and

cut off thofe paffions whereby any occafion is taken to break the law of my Gofpel, and have commanded that thofe things fhould be ftraitly obferved which do ftir up, purify, and ftrengthen the fpirit in all virtue and goodnefs. For they know that the fpirit could never be ftrong, and have the upper hand of the flefh, but by punifhing it, and by flying all occafions of evil. For when the fpirit is ftrengthened there will be always in you a chafter, a more fervent, and a more conftant love or devotion to keep my commandments. And it is evident that thefe holy fervants of mine, for this caufe had a will to appoint all things in fuch fort as might be for the furtherance of men in following the courfe of my Gofpel, and would not permit the fmalleft tittle that might be againft the rule thereof.

4. It appeareth manifeftly alfo that fome which lived after them added new conftitutions and many ceremonies to thefe rules, and do more feverely and fharply punifh men for their tranfgreffion of thefe ceremonies than of my Gofpel, which is a very prepofterous courfe, and contrary to all

good order. For a man is reprehended and punifhed if he fpeak out of time, if he fing out of tune, or if he offend in any of thefe ceremonies. But I had rather (although I allow of thefe) that there fhould not be fmaller but much greater care had of Evangelical precepts than of thefe ceremonies, and that there fhould be a fharper cenfure againft thofe that break my commandment than againft fuch as offend in thefe ceremonies. As for example, I would not have them go unpunifhed which fwear by my name, which backbite any body, which hate their neighbours, or do any fuch thing as my Gofpel doth forbid. For there muft needs be appointed fharper difcipline, and there muft always be feverer laws ordained and appointed to punifh thofe which do break my commandments; and for the obfervation whereof, the ancient fathers in times heretofore did prefcribe fundry rules. But what fhall I fay? I fee that you in thefe days do neither obferve my Gofpel nor yet the rules of the ancient fathers. You boaft of my words in your mouth, and of my Gofpel in your common talk, but it appeareth manifeſtly how far I am from your heart, ſeeing you do not love me nor my commandments.

5. Return you, therefore, now (although it be late) who have walked ſo long in crooked paths with your hearts unto me; do penance, and believe in my Goſpel, and do not only believe whatſoever my Goſpel teacheth, but by believing it, and loving it, do whatſoever it commandeth. If you will be Chriſtians, if you will be my Diſciples, imitate me, learn of me, becauſe I am weak and humble of heart; walk ye as I have walked. Moreover, if you will be Monks, if you will be Prieſts, or if you will be Religious men, do thoſe things which are of the ſpirit, and mortify by the ſpirit the works of the fleſh. If you be (as you ſay) Evangelical, and followers of my Goſpel, do thoſe things which my Goſpel doth command you; how long will you ſay unto me, Lord, Lord, and will not do thoſe things which I ſay? Do thoſe things which I command you, and ſhew yourſelves to be my friends, not in words only, but in deed and in truth, for he that heareth

To the Faithful Soul. 245

my words, he that hath my commandments and doeth them, this is he that loveth me.

6. And for ſtirring up again that fervent zeal which hath been heretofore in men's minds, and for renewing the obfervance of my Gofpel, which is almoſt worn out of ufe, I deliver now unto thofe who are my friends, and devoutly affected towards me, two very ſhort rules. Whereof the one is very fit for fuch as be lefs perfect, and but new beginners in following of my fervice; and the other for fuch as are more perfect, and defire with all earneſtnefs to attain to a moſt chaſte love of me. Wherein there is taught no heap of ceremonies, or multitude of prayers, but a reformation of the confcience and inward man, and a devotion of the mind. There is nothing entreated of touching the colour or faſhion of garments, but the defires and endeavours of men are ſtirred up to the honouring and following of Evangelical obedience. And there is one kind of fraternity made and fet down in this place, whereby the minds of many may be united in one, and the intents of all fuch agree in one, as do love and ferve me.

No man is here of neceffity bound to vow the obfervance of thofe things (although that a vow doth very much adorn, ftrengthen, and enrich a good will), neither yet doth it make a man, if men offend therein, farther guilty of a fault than the tranfgreffion of my law doth pronounce him.

7. But I do give a Law to all thofe that defire to ferve me, agreeable to every man's ability, and I do temper it in fuch fort as every man, being affifted by my grace, may keep and fulfil it. For my will is that all men fhould be faved, and I have furthered them by my help unto it, fo far as it was my good will and pleafure. And in this refpect I do often forbear finners, and wink at their infirmities that are weak, left I fhould break afunder a broken reed, or fhould extinguifh or altogether put out fmoking wood. And therefore, being defirous to gather together unto me all thofe that ferve me, I have divided them into two kinds. In the firft, I place thofe that be weak and new beginners; and in the fecond, thofe that be more perfect and long-practifed in my fervice; and I have fet down

such precepts for them both as I have chosen out of my Gospel, and are most agreeable to their state and vocation.

An Instruction or

Rule for such as be Weak and Imperfect, and but New Beginners in my Service.

WHOSOEVER will vow himself to be one of my soldiers, and to fight in my warfare, and give me his promise in that behalf, if he cannot at the beginning beware of all sins, yet let him specially beware of mortal sins. If thou, therefore, desirest to be accounted in the number of my faithful servants, beware of sin, and cut off and fly all occasions of sinning. Eschew evil, and do good, for I will never enter into a wicked and malicious soul, neither will I dwell in a body subject to sin.

2. Never spare thy life or temporal goods, if it may either deliver or preserve thy neighbour's soul from mortal sin. For thou oughtest to esteem more any soul

whatsoever (for the salvation whereof I gave my life) than thy body or temporal goods, and I ought to be more precious in thine eyes, for whose honour thou doest it, than thy corporal or temporal life. Never give thy consent, therefore, to any sin, but specially to mortal sin, whether it be in thyself or another. Whatsoever thou wouldst not have done unto thyself do not unto another. Use no fraud, practise no deceit, do no injury. And if these things be offered thee, bear them with silence for my sake, or at the least, complain no otherwise of them than justly, and after a just and rightful manner. For I have commanded my servants to prosecute that justly which is just.

3. Never requite evil with evil, nor reproach with reproach, never repay wrong with wrong, but suffer all for the love of me, who, when I was railed on, did not rail again; when I suffered, did not threaten mine enemies, but did willingly submit myself to an unjust sentence. Do thou, therefore, in like sort, if thine enemy hunger, feed him; if he thirst, give him to drink. Thou oughtest to love thine enemy, and to

do good to those that hate thee, that thou mayest be the son of the Father that is in heaven, who doeth good not only to those who are good, but to the evil also. Be merciful as thy Father in heaven is merciful; give alms to thy neighbour, if thou hast ability, or bestow daily at the least one benefit or other upon him, or some good turn, or some service, or some work of mercy, or some deed of charity.

4. And thou oughtest faithfully to exercise thyself in this exercise, in taking of compassion, or succouring of thy neighbour. For whosoever is merciful towards another shall obtain mercy at my hands, and whosoever shall do anything to the least of my servants, whether it be good or evil, I will account it as done unto myself. If thou livest according to the flesh thou shalt die, but if thou dost mortify the works of the flesh with the spirit thou shalt live. Mortify, therefore, thy desires, thy senses, and thy members here upon earth, that thou mayest not do whatsoever thy carnal appetite doth provoke thee unto. Thou shouldst every day, at the least, no less than once withdraw,

restrain, and deny thy consent for my sake, to something which thou desirest or wherein thou delightest. And if there happen nothing that day wherein thou mayest bridle thine affection in this sort, yet do it for the love of me as occasion is offered, in barring thyself from having, feeling, seeing, or hearing somewhat which thou much desirest, or to which thy concupiscence and the curiosity of thy nature doth move thee. And although there is no other fruit to be reaped by it, yet deny thine own will in this point, and kill this desire in thee for the love of me. Thou must never swear, but being enforced by lawful authority for a matter of truth before a Judge; thou must never speak of my name in vain, or unprofitably, or make a lie at any time.

5. Either read or hear Mass every day if thy state or office will permit thee, and do it in the memory and honour of my charity, and of all my benefits which I have heretofore most abundantly and willingly poured upon men, and do daily from time to time bestow upon them. But if thou canst not hear Mass, say with the same intention

To the Faithful Soul. 251

the prayer which I taught my Difciples, and the falutation of the Angel to my bleffed Mother, and offer me up to my Father in thy heart, and with me all thofe good works which I and my fervants either do or have done for thee, and the univerfal Church.

6. Thou oughteft every month once at the leaft facramentally to confefs thy fins, and to receive the Sacrament of my bleffed Body, at the feaft of my Nativity, and Refurrection, at Pentecoft alfo, and at the Affumption of my Mother, and at the feaft of All-Saints, except living under fome vow or in fome Monaftery, thou be reftrained there by the rule of thy life to do the fame. Thou oughteft to adore me every day early in the morning, being One God in Trinity of Perfons, and to recommend thyfelf to my protection, and to pray that I would defend thee, and all the world from fin. He that is fo fimple as he cannot perform this, let him read with a devout intention a *Pater nofter* and an *Ave Maria*.

7. When thou haft no better mental exercifes, by internal meditation and by fome-

what that may kindle a more fervent zeal in thee, say every day in the honour of my Passion and my Wounds, five *Pater nosters* and so many *Ave Marias*. Moreover, say every week in the veneration and honour of my Mother a hundred and fifty *Ave Marias*, that is, three Rosaries, every Rosary containing in itself fifty.

8. Make also every day in the veneration and honour of the Sacrament of my blessed Body, two low curtsies, reverences, or adorations. One to give me thanks for that charity and benefits which I shewed towards thee in my Incarnation, Death and Passion, and in the institution of this Blessed Sacrament. Another to give me as much honour as lieth in thee, in recompense of that reproach which I suffered at their hands that receive my precious Body unworthily, and do handle it impurely. Thou must every day make two other adorations or curtsies, one to obtain the fruit which I, dying, procured for all men by my Passion, and by the effusion of my blood and loss of my life, and which I have a will that all men should be partakers of.

9. Thou muſt in this alſo pray that I may pour my grace ſo into the heart of every man, as they may receive the ſame virtue, efficacy, and fruit of my Paſſion, which, being upon the Croſs and ſuffering there, I wrought for them, and in ſuch abundant ſort as I by my death did offer it unto them. Thou muſt make another kind of curtſey, or ſome kind of humiliation of thyſelf in my preſence, to praiſe me and give me thanks for the effuſion of my Blood, and for all my mercies which I have at any time poured out, both upon the good and bad; and thou muſt pray for their converſion who are in damnable ſins, and for the reformation of the Church; they that cannot conceive thus much, let them ſay with a devout intention, two *Pater noſters* and two *Ave Marias*.

10. Thou muſt faſt every Friday, if infirmity, weakneſs, labour, neceſſity, travail, age, or ſome other reaſonable occaſion do not let or hinder thee. Or if it like thee better, thou mayeſt eat twice that day, ſo that it be temperately and very ſparingly, and that thou uſeſt no ſodden meat at ſup-

per, whereby thou mayeſt puniſh thy fleſh, at the leaſt a little, and bring thyſelf to bewail the bitterneſs of my Death and Paſſion. Learn diligently to know the commandments of my Goſpe land the precepts of my Church, and when thou haſt learned them do not break them, for the love of any earthly thing whatſoever.

Another Instruction

Or Rule for ſuch as, with a more fervent Zeal and Spirit, do earneſtly Labour to attain· to Perfection.

HAVE placed thoſe in this ſecond diviſion which, forgetting clean all things that are paſt, deſire ever to come to a better and more perfect courſe; and therefore this rule ſhall be for ſuch as, ſeeking to attain to true perfection, do covet with a longing mind to be made one with me, and wholly united unto me.

2. Wherefore, whoſoever thou be that deſireſt to ſerve me with thy whole heart,

and to pleafe me in all things, thou muft not with thy certain knowledge and deliberate judgment offend in any fin, although it be but venial; and thou muft defire inftantly at my hands, with moft humble and devout prayers, that I may keep and preferve thee from all kind of fin. Thou muft be holy as I am holy; thou muft be perfect as I am perfect; thou muft be holy, I fay, in my fight, and when thou art fo, thou muft remember that it is not of thyfelf but it proceedeth from me. Thou muft not think otherwife of thyfelf than of a moft wicked finner, that had infinite times deferved eternal damnation, if my moft benevolent and ever moft ready mercy had not been always at hand to preferve and deliver thee from it.

3. Walk in that vocation whereunto thou art called, and live according to the ftate and rule of thy vocation. Obferve diligently and perform faithfully whatfoever my holy Scripture commandeth thee, and whatfoever thou promifeft with thy mouth unto me. It is alfo thy duty, not only to enquire after my commandments, but to

seek to know my pleasure in all things, and to ask my counsel, and even with a certain earnest desire to follow and fulfil them both.

4. Lead a solitary life, being separated from all unnecessary businesses, from familiarity, and discourses with men, and give thyself to silence, solitariness, and prayer, as much as thy state will permit thee. My Apostle saith that the servant of God ought not to be contentious; contend thou not therefore in words. Abstain also from every idle word, but chiefly from all carnal and back-biting speeches; never speak anything, nor yet hear any thing, of those which be absent but that which is good. And although that it may sometime be done with a good intention to speak evil of him that is absent, yet never consent to speak or to hear evil of him, except the matter which is spoken of be most certain and apparent. And yet, if thou dost exceed in this, thou must not go away unpunished, but thou must enjoin some penance and punishment to thyself for thine offence.

5. Observe sobriety in meat and drink,

To the Faithful Soul.

and ufe all my creatures with temperance, that thou mayeft be made poor in fpirit with the love of me, delighting in no worldly thing whatfoever, but as a ftranger and wayfaring man. Look upon all things in this world with a pure and free heart, not fubject any way unto them, but as it were paffing lightly by them, not having any defire to remain with them.

6. Accuftom thyfelf to fhew all humility, meeknefs, benignity, and piety towards thy neighbours, remembering and beholding me in every man, and frame thyfelf to deal fo with them, as thou wouldft deal with me. For in truth I take any thing whatfoever thou doft to thy neighbour as done unto myfelf.

7. Thou oughteft to judge no man, nor yet intrude thyfelf to difpute, or to give thy judgment of other men's matters and confciences, whatfoever they be; except thou art appointed a judge by me, and fo by the virtue of thine office art to give thy judgment therein. And yet, notwithftanding, if thou fhalt fee any man offend, and doft hope to do him fome good by thine

S

admonition (or at the leaſt haſt no miſtruſt to make him commit more grievous ſins by thy reprehenſion) thou mayeſt courteouſly admoniſh him who doth ſin, earneſtly and gently entreating him, that he would be mindful of his own ſalvation and amend his fault. But if he ſeek to defend himſelf, and obſtinately contend with thee in maintaining of his doing, do not thou diſpute with him, except thou have hope by little and little to bring him to a better courſe; neither yet labour to defend thine own ſpeech when it is to no purpoſe, but give him place humbly, without any anger and with all meekneſs and quietneſs.

8. Likewiſe, if thou art reprehended at any time without a cauſe, thou mayeſt, if thou wilt, gently and mildly give an account of thy dealing, but thou ſhalt do better (except any ſcandal might ariſe thereby) if thou doſt humbly aſk pardon, and without any excuſing of thyſelf promiſe amendment (as far as thou mayeſt lawfully do without offending of me) and withal thou mayeſt give him thanks to ſhew thy charity who did in this ſort admoniſh thee.

9. I have heretofore warned men in my Goſpel, that if any man will come after me he muſt deny himſelf. For as in the denying of a man's ſelf the whole perfection of a man's life confiſteth, ſo by the love of a man's ſelf he cometh ever to ruin and deſtruction. Labour, therefore, by all the means that thou mayeſt, for the utter denying of thyſelf, and let it be thy principal ſtudy how to mortify thine own will in thee. Thou muſt ſo diſpoſe of all thine own matters as thou mayeſt be ready either to do or omit things, in ſuch ſort as thou ſhalt be counſelled and adviſed by ſome good man, or one that feareth God, if thou haſt not a ſpiritual governor.

10. Truſt not thine own judgment in any thing. Do nothing of thine own head, chiefly in doubtful things where there may be danger. And therefore thou muſt not procure for thyſelf any thing in ſeeking to pleaſe thine own appetite (except ſuch things only as do manifeſtly appear without all doubt to be acceptable unto me), but thou muſt rather reſpect the profit of many, and thou muſt ever prefer before all things

my honour, and commit thyself wholly to my Providence. I will take care of thee, I will take the charge upon myself to provide for thee; and let this be thine only study, to behave thyself in such sort as thou do nothing to the derogation of my honour, and the resisting of my good pleasure.

11. But to the end that thy work may be more pleasing unto me, by the denying of thyself (if thou livest not in the monastic course of life) thou mayest for the undertaking and performance of this course promise thy obedience herein to a Priest or some other man that feareth me; neither ought the infelicity of this present age, nor the impiety of wicked men, which do slander and impugn vows and promises made unto God, yea even such as are most profitable for man's salvation, either move or discourage thee any whit. But thou oughtest to be the rather induced by this to rely thyself upon my mercy, and firmly to believe that I, who have given thee an aspiration to have a will to do well, and to make a holy vow, will also give thee power and

ability to fulfil it. For neither of them proceed from thyſelf, but it cometh from my grace both to have a will to do well, and to do well indeed, and both to promiſe and perform thoſe things which are profitable for thy ſalvation.

12. Chooſe a place that is ſecret, and deſire to live hid and unknown, and diſcloſe not thy counſels to every body, but to him only who is the director and guide of thy conſcience. Be not careful or deſirous to pleaſe men, ſeek not for their commendation, or to have a name amongſt them, neither yet ſtudy to do any thing whereby thou mayeſt obtain a great opinion, praiſe, or admiration amongſt them, ſeeing that all things are proper to me only, to which any praiſe or commendation is due. But endeavour rather ſo to bridle thine affections as that thou mayeſt, in all ſimplicity and purity of heart, think worſe and more baſely of thyſelf than of any other, and be deſirous that other men ſhould conceive the like opinion of thee. So as whatſoever thou doſt, whether it be a thing worthy of commendation, or elſe ſuch a thing as

may make thee to be contemned and reproached of others, be no more moved with it (if it be not ſin) either inwardly in thy mind, or outwardly in thy ſhew, by entering into any paſſion, than thou wouldſt be if any other man had done the ſame.

13. Boaſt nothing of thyſelf, glory nothing in thyſelf, challenge and aſcribe nothing to thyſelf, by the means of my gifts, attribute no more to thyſelf for any virtue that is in thee, or for any good works that are done by thy means, than thou wouldſt do to a hatchet or any other inſtrument, which is nothing at all in itſelf, and is able to do nothing by itſelf, but if any thing be done by it, it is by the will of the Artificer who worketh with it, and who could do the ſame by another inſtrument if it pleaſed him. For in that it is come to be an inſtrument, and that it hath any thing in itſelf whereby it may now be employed to ſome uſe, it hath not this ability of itſelf, nor from any other, but from the Artificer, who did frame it in ſuch ſort as it may work and do ſomewhat. But with-

To the Faithful Soul. 263

out an Artificer, or one to work with it, it lieth ſtill unprofitable, and ſerveth to no purpoſe.

14. In like ſort muſt he think of himſelf who deſireth to be my ſon and to imitate my humility, and will undertake to follow this rule of life; he muſt conſider of his own eſtate, how full he is of miſeries, defeꞓts, ſins, and infirmities. Moreover, he ought to look into every man, and reſpeꞓt thoſe things only in them wherein I have adorned them with any grace and virtue, that he may be brought by this conſideration to acknowledge himſelf always inferior unto them all. And let him not challenge or aſcribe any thing unto himſelf for thoſe virtues, operations, and good gifts, which I beſtow upon him; but let him make no other account of them than if they were in another, and let him give the praiſe and glory of them all unto me wholly, without challenging of any thing to himſelf thereby.

15. And therefore thou which deſireſt to be a follower of this rule muſt have great care of thyſelf, and thou muſt ſo diligently

look into thine own behaviour, and be so watchful in all thy actions, as thou neither mayest seek any thing, nor bend thyself to desire or follow any thing besides me; that is, thou must desire nothing but my glory, and the fulfilling of my pleasure only. Wherefore, in what thing soever thou findest thyself to bear rule, that is, in what thing soever thou seekest to please thyself, or findest self-love to reign in thee, there thou must renounce thyself, and omit wholly the doing of that thing (if thou hast no lawful impediment to the contrary) seeing by it thou didst not seek to please me with a pure intention.

16. Thou must complain to no man of those crosses which thou sufferest, except it be to have counsel at their hands; for thou oughtest to receive all things thankfully which I send thee, and to refer all things unto me. Therefore, howsoever the storms of affliction shall violently assail thee, or in what sort soever adversity shall chance to overwhelm thee, have thou a mind ever ready to endure all patiently, being wholly subject to me, and for me to all creatures.

Endeavour with violence to reprefs thefe motions which rife up againft thee, and labour clean to forfake thyfelf, and be not moved with any paffion againft men, neither yet contend, difpute, or refift them.

17. Seek not, moreover, means to avoid afflictions, nor to deliver thyfelf from them, but be content to receive all things with filence, in peace and tranquillity, and with an indifferent mind, as willing to receive adverfity as profperity at my hands. And be content to bear them with all quietnefs in thy foul, as long as it fhall be my pleafure. And when thou art in adverfity, do not feek with a deliberate intention, that is, of fet purpofe, for any confolation, though it be never fo little, but commit all things unto me, and patiently expect the event, and end of all things from my hands.

18. Thou muft confefs thy fins facramentally to a Prieft every week no lefs than once, but thou muft do it to me every day in prayer, and that very often, with the forrow of thy heart, and with an humble accufation of thyfelf for thy manifold offences; and thou muft offer thyfelf unto

me ready in all things to fet forth my glory, and to fulfil my pleafure.

19. Thou muft receive alfo the Sacrament of my Bleffed Body every month, once at the leaft, if thou canft not every week once or twice, and thou muft not omit to make thofe curtfies which I fet down in the former rule in the veneration of my glorious Sacrament, and in the memory of my death. If thou fhalt fail in any of thefe things heretofore recited, thou fhalt not thereby be guilty of a new fault by undertaking the performance of this rule, neither fhalt thou offend more by the means of it, than another which liveth without this rule and fraternity; but for every tranfgreffion which thou makeft by being overcome with thine own inconftancy, do not ceafe altogether from following this good purpofe of thine, but enjoin thyfelf for thy penance and punifhment to fay one *Ave Maria*, or fome greater penance, as thou fhalt think convenient. Thou muft fay every night, notwithftanding, three *Ave Marias* before my moft holy and glorious Mother. One for thofe negligences which

thou haſt ignorantly committed, and which thou doſt not remember. Another, to entreat me by her interceſſion for the amendment of thy life, perſeverance in virtue, and obtaining of my grace. The third, that the worſhipping and honouring of me may be daily amplified, enlarged, augmented, and increaſed, either by this rule or by what other means ſoever that ſhall ſeem beſt unto me.

20. Uſe ſuch ſpiritual exerciſes as are moſt agreeable to thy devotion, ſtate, and nature, wherein thou mayeſt ſpend thy time profitably, and be lifted by them in thy heart unto me, increaſing daily in goodneſs, and enforcing thyſelf from time to time to do better and better. He that will undertake to follow this fraternity or rule, and govern himſelf according to the preſcript order thereof, let him kneel before the image of me crucified, if he be alone or had rather be ſecret by himſelf, and let him earneſtly entreat me that I will vouchſafe to receive him for my diſciple, that I will pour my grace upon him, and both ſtrengthen and confirm this good will in

him so fully, as he may resolve constantly, and unremovably, to live according to these rules and directions. Let him also teach others, and gain souls unto me, and bring them unto my service. But if there be many that undertake to follow these rules, they may exhort one another in me, and may be united in brotherly charity, by the means of the likeness and unity they have in their course of life, in that they all do follow this fraternity. And let them not receive every man at all adventures into their society, especially such as there is no hope of the constancy of their mind, and perseverance of devotion, left that their lightness and instability, which do not endeavour to attain to the perfection of that course they have undertaken, may discourage others in their good purpose, and make them give over their holy intention.

Verses for Helping

A Man's Memory, wherein are expreſſed the Principal and Moſt Special Points of thoſe Good Leſſons which are comprehended in theſe Rules.

> Have ſpecial care to rule thy tongue;
> Forbear to pleaſe thy carnal will;
> Do good to all, while time thou haſt,
> And what thou art remember ſtill.
>
> Forſake thyſelf, it is not much,
> Chriſt took for thee much greater pain;
> Be meek in mind, that thou with Him
> In endleſs glory may'ſt remain.

Y the rule of thy tongue is underſtood, that thou muſt refrain from all idle, back-biting, contentious and quarrelling words, and from all complaining ſpeeches. By forbearing to pleaſe thy will, is meant that thou muſt wean thyſelf from the deſire of all vain pleaſures, tranſitory things, and earthly delights, and that thou muſt mortify all thy ſenſes. By doing good to every man, thou art exhorted to perform all the

works of mercy and charity towards thy neighbours. And in that thou art willed to remember what thou art, it is to make thee know thyself, and to humble thee, because if thou look into thine own ability, thou shalt plainly find that thou art merely nothing of thyself, nor yet able by thyself to do anything at all.

By forsaking of thyself is meant, that thou must renounce thine own will, deny thine own self, and seek to please God only, and wholly with a pure intention. Lastly, thou art exhorted to be meek in mind, whereby is signified that thou must use all meekness, courtesy, and benignity towards thy neighbours, and thou must ever retain all peace, quietness, and tranquillity in thy soul, patiently expecting the pleasure of Almighty God and accepting always in the best part of His providence, whatsoever it shall be His will to send thee.

CHRISTO LAUDES ET SANCTÆ MATRI EJUS HONOR. AMEN.

A VERY SHORT EXERCISE OF LOVE TO GOD.

The Father, God the Son, and God the Holy Ghoſt, the Moſt Bleſſed Trinity, and one true God, wherewith a Man ought once every day to offer himſelf with his whole Soul unto his Divine Majeſty, and to give Him moſt humble Thanks for all the Benefits which he hath received at His moſt gracious hands.

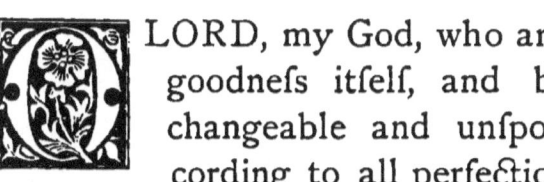LORD, my God, who art infinite goodneſs itſelf, and both unchangeable and unſpotted according to all perfections which I can conceive of Thee, always remaining the very same that Thou wert from the beginning. Thou madeſt every creature for Thy glory, Thou doſt preſerve and govern them with ſuch wiſdom that, being ſo many, so great, and ſo divers as they are, there is none which doth withdraw himſelf

from being under Thy subjection, and yet thou dost neither dig nor labour, but always remainest in most blessed quiet. Thou hast created me according to Thine own image and likeness, and dost preserve me in that being which I am. Thou hast redeemed me of most pure charity by the death of Thy most Blessed Son, and in most painful and troublesome manner, that Thou mightest shew unto me the riches of Thy grace, the bounty of Thy mercy, and the exceedingness of Thy love towards me. Thou hast made me to come in a noble sort to the acknowledging of Thy most holy name, Thou hast brought me to that most Holy Religion, and Thou hast raised me to so high a dignity. Thou hast directed me always in Thine own presence, and hast carried a special regard towards me, and Thou hast made me to find favour in the eyes of Thy servants, that they might take care of my salvation.

2. Thou hast delivered me also from many dangers and tribulations, both of body and soul, from infirmities, from sicknesses, from beggary, from fallings head-

long, from fundry perils, from wicked men, from drowning, and from infinite other mifchiefs which might have happened to me as well as to others, if Thy love and mercy had not delivered me from them. Thou haft alfo moft often delivered me from fin, from falling into the gulf of finners, from being devoured by them, and from eternal damnation. Thou haft, moreover, given me a firm confidence to believe that Thou haft chofen me to eternal happinefs, wherein Thou wilt manifeft Thine own felf unto me. Oh, I fhall then plainly know and fee Thee, my Lord and God; I fhall love Thee perfectly and moft purely; I fhall find moft bleffed peace in enjoying Thee only; and I fhall always moft fincerely praife and glorify Thee with all Thy Saints. O merciful God, confirm this, and perform this quickly in me. O Lord, my God, for all the benefits that Thou haft wrought, and fhall work in me, and in every one of Thy creatures, be all honour, glory, thanks, dutiful fervice, hearty affection, chafte fear, and fincere love to Thy Divine Majefty, world without end, *Amen.*

T

3. O merciful God, make me thankful, and pardon me, I beseech Thee most graciously, for all those abominable ingratitudes, intolerable negligences, and innumerable sins, which I have committed against Thee, *(and if thou haſt communicated thou mayeſt add to this and ſay,)* for Thine own sake, and by the virtue of Thy Blessed Sacrament which I have received, root out of my heart all malice, grant me an humble confession, a hearty sorrow, a discreet abhorring, a zealous forsaking and a necessary detestation of all my sins, and both true repentance and a perfect amendment in this life. Grant, also, that I may never again offend Thee, for Thine unspeakable mercy and infinite goodness, and make me to love with all the affection that it is possible for me Thy most sweet friendship, and Thy most precious grace; excite me most earnestly to desire it, and quickly to find it, with perseverance therein even to the end. O merciful God, grant that I may not neglect this goodness and long-suffering of Thine. Strengthen me always, both in soul and body, to do Thee service, and grant me Thy grace that I may

To the Faithful Soul. 275

foberly ufe Thy creatures, to the glory and praife of Thy name.

4. I give Thee thanks, O Lord Jefu, and Thee, O Holy Ghoft, being equal with the eternal Father, which wert content, for my falvation, to be conceived of the fame Holy Ghoft, and to be born of the moft pure Virgin Mary, and to be made man. What do I owe Thee, and how much am I bound unto Thee, O Lord Jefu? O God, who wert man; O man, who wert God; O Meffias; O Chrift, the anointed of our Lord; O Emmanuel; O God with us; O Lord of exceeding Majefty, and moft conftant Lover of men, how wert Thou made a mortal man, fubject to a mortal life, to fheddings of Thy blood, to perfecutions, to forrow, to pains, and chiefly to the torments of the Crofs, when Thou wert made poor and miferable, and moft vile and contemptible in the fight of all men! What fhall I render unto Thee, O fweet Lover, for that moft bitter death which Thou fufferedft for me, and for that unfpeakable charity which Thou fhewedft towards me?

5. I befeech Thee, O Lord Jefus, by Thy

Incarnation, by Thy remaining in the Virgin's womb; by the joy of Thy foul, at the grace of Thine union, when Thy divinity and humanity were joined in one; by Thy Nativity in winter-time, by the pain of Thy Circumcifion, by the veneration wherewith the Sages did adore Thee, by Thy prefentation in the temple, by Thy flight into *Egypt*, by Thy banifhment there, by Thy fearful return again into Thine own country; by Thy fubjection, obedience, and moft virtuous life; by the penance which Thou didft for our fins; by Thy baptifm, fafting, and temptation in the wildernefs; by Thy penury, poverty, and neceffity which Thou enduredft in this mortal life; by all the troubles which Thou feltft; by Thy moft gracious virtues, and glorious life; by that ingratitude which Thou didft endure at the Jews' hands, when they would have thrown Thee down headlong from the top of the hill; when they fought traitoroufly to entrap Thee in Thy words and deeds, and when they did devife how to ftone Thee with their violent hands.

6. I befeech Thee, alfo, by Thy modefty,

humility, patience, meekneſs, and all the other virtues; by the humiliation of Thyſelf at Thy diſciples' feet, when Thou waſhedſt them; by the inſtitution of the moſt Bleſſed Sacrament of Thy precious Body, and by the moſt delightful taſte and unſpeakable ſweetneſs thereof; by Thy ſadneſs, agony, and bloody ſweat which Thou didſt endure, when Thou prayedſt in the garden; by Thy being forſaken of Thy diſciples and all men; by Thy being betrayed by Thy own ſervant; by the bands, reproaches, injuries, buffets, blows, ſpitting upon, and blaſphemies which Thou didſt ſuffer; by the falſe accuſation and unjuſt condemnation which Thou receivedſt; by Thy grief for *S. Peter's* denying Thee, *Judas* betraying Thee, and the other diſciples forſaking Thee; by Thy being led unto divers Judges, to receive the ſentence of death; by the mockery, nakedneſs, ſcourging of Thy body, crowning of Thy head, and vexing of Thy innocent ſoul; by Thy being rejected when *Barabbas* was accepted; by the unjuſt ſentence of the Judge; by Thy being led with thieves; by the carrying of Thy Croſs; by the mockery of Thy adverfaries, and by the fhamefulnefs of Thy death; by the lamentation which devout perfons, but chiefly Thy Mother, made for Thee; by the toil and wearinefs which Thou fuftained; by the bitter drink which Thou tafted; by the plucking of Thy flefh, with the plucking of Thy garments, which Thou endured; by Thy being ftretched out on the Crofs; by the nailing of Thee to the Crofs, and the torments which Thou there received; by thofe bleffed tears which Thou didft fhed; by thofe intolerable injuries which Thou didft patiently bear; by Thy moft holy prayer; by the commiferation which Thou tookeft of the thief that faid, "*Lord, remember me when Thou comeft into Thy kingdom.*"

7. By the compaffion of Thy Mother, by Thy crying Thou wert forfaken, by Thy drinking of vinegar and gall, by Thy faying all was finifhed, by Thy moft cruel death, by Thy unfpeakable charity wherewith Thou fufferedft it; by the piercing of Thy fide, Thy Mother looking on; by Thy holy burial, by the heavinefs of Thy friends for Thy death, by Thy refurrection, by Thy

appearing to them again, by Thy afcenfion, by the fending of the Holy Ghoft, by the inftitution and foundation of Thy Church, by the affumption of Thy Mother, by the glorification of Thy Saints, by Thy laft judgment, and by the eternal falvation which Thou wilt grant to Thy fervants' fouls and bodies. Thou didft rife again from death triumphantly, Thou didft appear to Thy Difciples glorioufly, Thou didft rejoice their hearts wonderfully, Thou didft afcend up into heaven in their fight miraculoufly, Thou didft fend the Holy Ghoft to direct Thy Church, Thou didft gather up Thy fervants unto Thee, Thou didft affume Thy bleffed Mother to Thy eternal kingdom, Thou fhalt come to judge the quick and the dead, Thou fhalt reign with all Thy Saints world without end; and let me remain with Thee, O fweet Jefu.

8. What fhall I render unto Thee, O gracious Lover, for that moft bitter death which Thou fufferedft for me, and for that unfpeakable charity which Thou fhewedft towards me? O good Jefus, make me, I befeech Thee, partaker of all Thy merits

and mercies, make me thankful for them, and in recompenfe of them to love Thee again who loved me fo much, and even to be ready to die for Thy love. Pardon me for all mine unworthinefs, all my vilenefs, all my undutifulness, and all my negligences, wherein I have offended Thee; teach me true wifdom, that Thou only mayeft be wifdom unto me, and all other things whatfoever foolifhnefs. Grant that I may never ufe any kind of concupifcence. Grant me true knowledge, pure intentions, holy purpofes, and perfect difcretion in my confcience, and in Thy holy fervice. Make me ftout and forward to fhew myfelf fuch an one in the fight of Thy glorious Majefty as becometh me. Encourage me and ftrengthen me againft all faintnefs of heart, errors, fcrupulofities, fancies, and fuch like.

9. Open my underftanding in judging truly of the Scriptures, and conceiving rightly of Thy good pleafure, that I may know what is acceptable in Thy fight, and when I do know it, grant that I may both love and perform it. Deliver me from taking any care for other men's caufes, or bufying my-

To the Faithful Soul. 281

felf with other men's matters, that by this means I may more wholly pleafe Thee, and more perfectly, fafely, and quickly come unto Thee. And if it fhall pleafe Thy moft excellent Majefty to work this in me, Thy will be done; and help me, I befeech Thee, that I may be a profitable member in all Offices touching Thy Service, and neglect nothing that may exprefs my duty towards Thee. Make me like unto Thee both in life and manners. Grant me modefty, humility, obedience, patience, and whatfoever elfe is neceffary for my vocation.

10. O moft gracious and loving Lord, quicken me and revive me with Thy grace, feparate me wholly from all evil, and convert me altogether unto Thyfelf, and grant that I may hate that which Thou hateft, and love that which Thou loveft. Make me to increafe continually and abundantly in all virtues. Strengthen me and confirm me in Thy Catholic Faith, truly underftood. Increafe faith in me, fettle and fortify in me an affured hope, grant me always to conceive rightly of Thee, and to rely wholly

upon Thee. Give me a firm confidence in Thee and that I may worſhip Thee devoutly, honour Thee chaſtely, and love Thee perfectly with a ſimple heart, a pure ſoul, a quiet mind, and a ſafe conſcience. Grant that Thou only mayeſt content me, that Thou only mayeſt delight me, and that Thou only mayeſt poſſeſs me; and that I may deſire Thee only, love Thee only, and ſtudy how to pleaſe Thee only. Make me that I may never be ſeparated from Thee, that I may labour earneſtly to come unto Thee, find peace in Thee alone, and quickly come unto Thee. Let all inordinate love be clean mortified in me, and remove all other impediments from me that may hinder me to come unto Thee, who art only to be deſired, and only to be beloved.

11. I do confeſs Thee, O Lord my God, three perſons, the Father, the Son, and the Holy Ghoſt; and I do adore and worſhip Thee, One true God, as Thou art in Thyſelf, ſubmitting and ſubjecting myſelf wholly and irrevocably to Thy moſt glorious Majeſty, as all creatures are bound to do, lying proſtrate at Thy feet to yield

themselves in everything unto Thee, readily with all good will, perfectly with all obedience, and truly with all sincerity.

12. Forgive me, O most merciful God, that I have not carried that affection towards thee which I ought, and grant me Thy grace, that I may worship Thee, reverence and love Thee in truth, and in such perfection as I am bound.

Christo Laudes et Sancta Matri Ejus Honor. Amen.

THE END.

LONDON:
PRINTED BY J. OGDEN AND CO.,
172, ST. JOHN STREET, E.C.

www.ingramcontent.com/pod-product-compliance
Lightning Source LLC
Chambersburg PA
CBHW032042230426
43672CB00009B/1439